The Computer Survival Handbook

The Computer Survival Handbook

How to Talk Back to Your Computer

by
Susan Wooldridge
and
Keith London

Gambit
INCORPORATED
Boston
1973

Contents

CONTENTS

Introduction

We were pressured into writing this book by some disgruntled businessmen—unhappy computer users. They didn't want the usual list of platitudes. They didn't want a dry text. They wanted a practical handbook of what to do when a computer system was being planned.

'The last thing I want is a computer. How do I stop them?'

'Those computer guys have messed up everything they've touched so far. What do I do when they start on me?'

'They get me every time. How can I stop them when I can't even understand what they're talking about?'

'I want to get those bastards. Just give me the ammunition and I'll do the rest.'

'I want to make the computer work for me, but how?'

'Help!'

And other less printable things.

'Traitors,' cried some of our computer colleagues, but we decided to write this book anyway. With twenty years in the computer business between us, we've seen a lot of mistakes and a few successes. We've worked with both computer users and computer technicians; we've seen both sides of the fence. We believe computers can make a valuable contribution to business, and to society.

We hope this book will entertain you, but our purpose in writing it was more ambitious than that. It is intended as a working brief for those who are convinced that it is possible to make the computer work for them, profitably, but don't know how. It's a way out of the trap for those who want to stop throwing away money on computer processing. It's a handbook for those shock troops of business who have been bent, torn or multilated by the company's computer, or who are afraid they might be.

To all of you who, though perhaps still bearing the scars of battles lost, are determined not to give up the war for survival against the computer, this book is dedicated.

Susan Wooldridge
Keith R. London

1

The Age of Automation

Computers have had a bad press. A polite way of saying it is that their reputation stinks. A lot of claims made for them have not come to pass; money has been wasted, invested in projects which gave nothing back; people's jobs have been changed, not always for the better.

Even though it's popular to knock computers, they're here to stay, and their impact on our daily lives is increasing all the time. You get up in the morning and your wife cooks your breakfast on a stove whose gas or electricity supply is controlled and billed by computer; you go out to the garage and get into your car which was designed and manufactured with the help of a computer; the traffic lights are computer controlled, and when you stop to buy gas which could not have been got out of the ground and processed without computers, you pay with a credit card and will be billed through a computerized accounting system. And you're not even at the office yet.

If you're the pessimistic type, you can say that the electricity bill is usually wrong, your computer-designed hub-caps have a tendency to detach themselves, the computer-assisted assembly-line forgot to give you *two* windshield-wipers, the half-hour traffic jam at the computer-controlled traffic lights is intolerable, and the credit card company takes three months to get your bill out (not mentioning the fact that the billing delay gives you extended free credit).

We attended a dinner recently where the speaker's theme was change, that necessity is the mother of invention, and war its father. The audience was mostly businessmen. The speaker listed the good things that came of the last world war, including penicillin and radar. He then went on to the bad things: the atomic bomb, advanced brain-washing techniques, computers . . . the audience roared. All except for one man who was an executive of a big computer manufacturer. As the guests were leaving he cornered the speaker. 'Your remark,' he said bluntly, 'was cheap. We both know computers are good for a quick laugh with any group of businessmen. Why didn't you mention putting a man on the moon, keeping the airlines in business, medical research . . .?'

'And what about the average businessman who was here tonight?' retorted the speaker, and then wished he hadn't. We left ten minutes later while the computer man was still reeling off his list of vague generalities: ' . . . better management information, faster decision-making, cheaper processing of information, staff reductions, better use of management resources, improved customer satisfaction . . .'

The multi-billion dollar computer industry was not built on failure and ridicule. As that executive pointed out, there have been some spectacular computer success stories. There have been some unspectacular successes, too; small companies expanding happily, clerical drudgery removed from jobs, even businesses saved through the use of computers. Unfortunately, the disasters are more newsworthy, and they happen regularly.

Computers, as we are often told, are only tools; it's how you use them that counts. If you try to spread butter with a hammer, you are using the wrong tool; if you are pounding a nail and mash your thumb, the fault is with the workman, not the tool.

Let's look at how computers can be used in business. Most organizations are trying to maximize profits, which means reducing costs and increasing revenue. A non-profit or public service company has an analogous aim—to give the best possible service at the lowest cost. To take costs first: every company has a major expenditure on staff; a computer can do the work of many clerks, or, as more often happens, do more work with the same number. A computer can help to run your machines better, to organize your warehouse and your transport more efficiently, to reduce investment in inventory. If your product is money—banks and mortgage brokers—the computer can do calculations faster and more accurately and handle more items of information than any human can. A computer can help to increase revenue, too, by making faster deliveries, organizing the inventory so as to reduce out-of-stocks, sending invoices out sooner, and increasing efficiency to get more work through the same number of machines. If you are in a rapidly expanding business, or one which has run into tough competition or financial trouble, the computer could be your only hope for survival.

That's all very well, you say, but what about those companies whose computers have put them into bankruptcy? The answer is that they were using the wrong tool, or using it the wrong way. Perhaps they should never have bought a computer in the first place; or it was a good idea, but they misused it. The fault was with the management, not the computer.

The age of automation is here. If you work in business, almost any business, your job will sooner or later be affected by a computer. Chances are that it has been already. You are not powerless; you can work *with* the computer, make it work for you; change potential disaster into one of those success stories, whether it be a personal or a business success, or both.

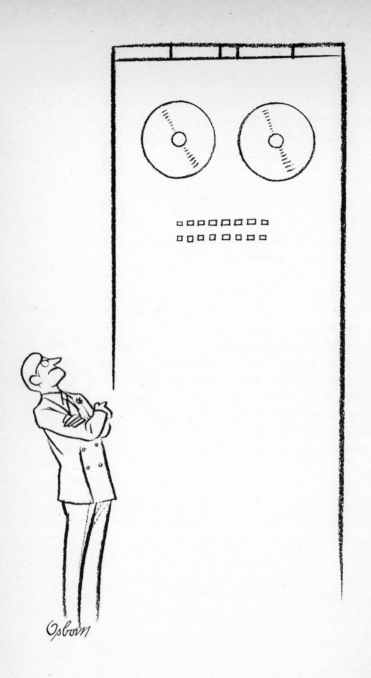

2

You and Them

This chapter is about attitudes toward computers, or more accurately, toward computer people and what they represent. Prepare you own list. Get your ideas out into the open and the remainder of the book can then be read with a purpose: to confirm or change your attitude, as you wish.

In a nutshell, the people in a company can be divided into two camps: *You* and *Them*. *You* is anybody in the company who may use computers; *them* are the people in the computer department. *You* will probably never become one of *them*; *they* have never been, are not, and will never be one of *you*.

Your attitude towards computers will probably be one of these:

— apathetic and undecided
— enthusiastically in favor
— embittered and against

Your feelings about a computer system for your department could be:

— of course we want one!
— over my dead body
— an open mind

What determines your attitude? There are a million possible reasons. A representative selection is given below:

Against computers

1. You have read horror stories in the press, and in books like this one.
2. Your father was out of work in the depression; this has scarred you for life because computers=automation=unemployment.
3. You mistrust things you don't understand.
4. You're afraid you'll lose control.
5. You have seen *them* (the computer department) botch up all the projects tackled to date, and you're afraid they'll do the same with yours.

For computers

1. You want to seem modern and dynamic.
2. It was your idea in the first place that the company get a computer.
3. Your son, brother, or uncle is a computer salesman.
4. You bought ten IBM shares in the thirties and you're now a millionaire.
5. You've seen *them* botch up all their projects so far and you're hoping they'll do the same with yours; it will cover up all your mistakes.

You also have to look at your possible attitudes toward *them*. *They* are:

1. A group of dedicated technicians, working in a dynamic new field to better the performance of all parts of the company and the company as a whole.
2. Long-haired, introverted backroom boys, totally out of touch with real life.

3. They're here today and gone tomorrow; they stay such a short time you can never get to know them.

4. The computer manager? A power-seeker furthering his own ends on the theory that he who controls the data controls the company. (Watch out, that theory may be right.)

List out your own feelings. (For survival, keep that list under lock and key; *they* seem to be everywhere.)

And how do you think that they see you? (To *them*, *you* are *them* and *they* are *you*, of course.)

1. They aren't strictly necessary, of course, for running the company.

2. They're like Columbus, when it comes to computer systems. They start off not knowing where they're going, arrive not knowing where they are, and return not knowing where they've been.

3. Profits? Cash flow? Management by objectives? That has nothing to do with me—I'm on the computer side.

4. They're OK as long as they don't interfere.

5. Just let us have a chance to take over their jobs, then we'll get somewhere with this company.

6. Who?

Whatever your attitude about computers and *them*, if you work in business you will eventually become involved with computers. You may do it by choice, you may be pressured from above or by *them*, or it may be a normal case of the creeping automation syndrome.

INFLUENCE AND INFILTRATION

An insidious infiltration movement, some say, is trying to change *them* into *you* and *you* into *them*. The theory:

— *You* will bring *them* down to commercial
  earth, and get systems which fit the
  business.
— *They* will spread the gospel among *you*.

We were giving a presentation to the top management of a very large oil company. 'Tell me,' said the vice-president, 'the characteristics of the users who would make the best systems people.' He listened to the list of attributes: 'Bah,' he said, 'you've just described my best managers and potential managers. And you expect me to release them to the computer department!'

Imagine a future, the pundits say, in which a new generation of managers, who have been brought up with computers, takes the reins. Utopia. But it hasn't happened so far.

In one company the movement of systems people to user departments was carefully planned early in the life of the computer installation. But it hasn't been entirely successful because:

— They were getting paid more in the computer department, and who wants a cut?
— They had seen some of the user departments in action, and wouldn't work there for any amount of money.
— They had a wide brief to deal with most parts of the company, and didn't want to settle down.
— They said their career is in data processing, not in production, accounts or sales.

Still, there are benefits to be realized. How well the trend works in practice, we'll have to wait some time to see.

A better solution might be to require a systems analyst to work in your department for a few weeks before he designs a computer system for you. This could *not* take the place of a formal investigation, as we shall see later, but it would give him some idea of what the company does.

3

The Jargon Barrier—Phase I

Half the battle of understanding computers—and more important, computer people—is to understand the jargon. If you really want to come to terms with them, you will have to understand their in-jokes and their pompous way of talking. For example, we once heard a computer man start off a speech with a joke that required at least five years' experience to understand. Later he said: 'We have outlined the opportunity areas; now to solutionize them for you.' Translated it meant: 'They're the problems, now the solution.' As with any technical area, computer people have developed their own special terminology and slang. This puts a barrier between you and them which must be overcome.* Equally, you must be careful not to use an out-of-date term or mispell a technical word; it immediately identifies you as a gauche outsider who is trying just a little too hard: for example, using 'programme' rather than 'program' to mean computer instructions, or 'hardware' rather than 'software'. This chapter introduces you to some of the simpler terms in computer usage.

First, some of the jobs in data processing:

* The barrier is not unique to you and them. At a party recently, we listened to a conversation between two computer technicians. We couldn't understand a word. When they went off to join different groups, we approached them separately to ask what they had been talking about. They hadn't even understood each other!

Data processing manager: His job is self-evident. He runs the whole department, usually including the operation of the computer; but the biggest part of his job is concerned with developing new systems, and then keeping them running. The casualty rate among DPMs is high, because they get two sorts of problems— all their own staff's gripes, plus complaints from everyone else in the company having computer problems.

Systems analyst: The person whose job it is to define a data-processing problem, design a computer system to solve it, and hold your hand while it's implemented. Almost immediately he has to work on changing the system to improve it, make it do what you *really* want, or get it to conform to a new tax law just passed.

Programmer: A person whose job it is to design, write, and test programs, the instructions which get the computer to do a specific job. Experts theorize that, through evolution and in-breeding, programmers may become a distinct sub-species of the human race.

You shouldn't have too much trouble differentiating between the last two; look at their appearance and their apparent contact with reality and you can *see* the difference. However, if you really are stuck, then try asking the analyst or programmer how he would tell the sex of a parrot. The true programmer will reply, with impeccable logic, that he would teach it to talk and then ask it. The analyst, of course, will learn its language and then ask it. Some companies combine the jobs of programming and systems analysis and give them to the same man, called variously a *programmer/analyst*, a *progalyst*, or an *anagrammer*.

Now to the 'wares' of computing:

Hardware: Any item of equipment; specifically, the computer, including all on-line peripherals and black boxes (described below).

Software: In its widest sense, any program. Usually used in a more restricted context to mean programs for performing common, general tasks, for example sorting records. Software can be bought or leased from an outside supplier, just as hardware is.

Firmware: Jargoneers' term for software which is so basic it would be impossible to operate the computer without it and which can, therefore, be thought of as being part of the machine.

Liveware: Revolting (and misleading) expression meaning computer people.

A few more terms dealing with hardware, beginning with the two major parts of the computer:

CPU: *C*entral *P*rocessor *U*nit, also known as the *mainframe*. The guts of the computer, the part that does arithmetic, logical comparisons, holds the data while it's processed, and holds the programs. The blackest of all black boxes.

Peripherals: Units which are attached by cables to the CPU. Used to get data in, data out, and act as a reservoir for large amounts of data which cannot be held in the CPU at one time (for example, mass data storage devices which hold commercial files). The card reader, typewriter, disk storage device, and magnetic tape units are all peripherals.

Equipment and activities can be in one of two states:

On-line: Devices which are physically connected to the computer; or a job which is done by the computer. An on-line device, however, need not be physically in the same room or even the same building as the CPU. (See *Terminal* below.)

Off-line: A device not connected to the computer, or a job not performed by the computer. For example, if a peripheral is disconnected from the CPU for repairs, it goes from 'on-line' to 'off-line'.

Back to hardware and the CPU:

Memory: Part of the CPU used to store data and programs during processing. The fastest but most expensive way of holding and gaining access to data in the computer. Also known as:

Core: Now an obsolete term. Derives from the tiny magnetic cores which were used in older computers. Still used by conservative people working on older machines.

Bit: The smallest unit of storage, described in the text books as: 'a contraction of the terms binary digit, pertaining to a digit, 0 or 1, in binary notation using radix 2'. If you want to follow this one up, then look in the said text books. Six, seven, or eight bits are used to represent one character (a digit o to 9, an alphabetic character A through to Z, a special symbol $+*/@$()$? etc).

Byte: A position in memory which consists of a group of eight bits. One byte can hold a character (one value in the range o to 9, A to Z, *+ etc).

Word: Another way of grouping bits (and bytes) in computer memory. May be of a fixed number of bits, such as four bytes (thirty-two bits), or it may be of a variable length, depending on the type of computer.*

From the CPU we can now turn to some more terminology concerned with the peripherals. Peripherals can be grouped into three classes:

Input: Devices which are used to get information into the CPU from the human user. Some means of input require a keyboard transcription to get them from the written form into computer input form. Examples are:

— punched cards
— paper tape
— magnetic tape

Other forms of input are documents which can be read directly by the input device. These include specially pre-printed characters (MICR—magnetic-ink character recognition and OCR—optical character recognition) such as appear on the bottom of a check. Lastly there are direct input devices, which afford the user immediate access to the CPU: typewriter terminals, special keyboard units fitted to visual display devices (like television screens), acoustic character recognition (voice input). These are only some of the input devices available; new methods and devices are brought on to the market every day.

Output: Devices which put information out for human consump-

---

* Claimed to be the only *true* way of arranging computer memory from the text: 'In the beginning there was The Word and The Word was four bytes long . . .'

tion. Examples are the line-printers (which can produce miles of reports), graph-plotters, visual display screens, typewriters.

File storage: Devices which can hold a reservoir of mass data within the computer system. They are on-line to the CPU, and selected information can be put on the file or retrieved from the file. Examples are:

Magnetic tape: Plastic tape coated with a magnetizable layer for recording data by the computer. Data is recorded on the tape in the form of tiny 'blips' of magnetism. A tape once recorded can be stored in an off-line library and read into the computer when required. The peripheral used for reading or writing the tape is called variously a *tape drive*, *tape deck*, *tape transport*, or *tape unit*.

Magnetic disk: A storage device in which data is recorded on concentric tracks on magnetic-coated platters. Often incorrectly described as being like an automatic record-player.

Magnetic cards and strips: Forget them; other than some very special devices (such as the National Cash Register CRAM), most of these devices have been withdrawn officially or unofficially from the market.

Terminal: An input/output peripheral device which is on-line to the computer, but which is in a remote location: another room, another city, or another country.

Peripherals are connected to the CPU via *control units*.

The last group of hardware terms are concerned with the time computer operations take and are generally used by computer technicians in an attempt to overwhelm you:

Millisecond: One thousandth of a second; abbreviated as ms and pronounced with gusto as 'millisec'.

Microsecond: One millionth of a second; abbreviated as μs (and sometimes pronounced as 'musec'). In speech, abbreviated to 'mike' by determined jargoneers, as in 'this will only take a mike'.

Nanosecond: One-thousand-millionth of a second, abbreviated as ns. Easily remembered because it has nine zeros. Usually pronounced only by engineers.

The selection of the appropriate term is important if you want to get the right emphasis. Suppose a particular operation on the computer is going to take .065 seconds.

— 'It will take 65 millisecs' (size of figure implies speed).
— 'It will take 6,500 mikes' (size of figure implies slowness).
— 'It will take over six million nanos' (with derision).

There is a plethora of specialized programming terms which would fill a handbook on their own. Only the most basic terms are described below. There is a full chapter on programming later in the book. First, the basic product:

Program: Noun: a series of coded instructions which gets the computer to perform a particular job. These instructions are loaded into and stored within the CPU and obeyed one by one. Each instruction dictates to the computer that a specific operation be performed: add two numbers together, read more input information, fetch a file record, print a line on a report, and so on. In this respect a computer is a moron. It will perform only those operations it is specifically told to do. The programmer's job is, in essence, to take what might be a complex program and break it down into a very simple step-by-step series of instructions which can be performed by a computer. Verb: to design, code, and test a series of instructions. In Britain, often mispelled as programme.

Here are some of the expressions you might hear programmers using:

Bug: An error in a computer program. Hence the term 'debugging', meaning to locate and erradicate errors. Hence 'debuggers', meaning certain programmers who are good at it.

Loop: A way of arranging instructions in a computer program. By using a special type of instruction, a branch instruction, a series of computer actions can be repeated until a certain condition is met, such as when all the lines of a report have been printed. See *Closed loop*.

Closed loop: A loop which is completely circular. Sometimes it is the result of a program bug, so that the condition which will terminate a loop is never met; the computer will perform the instructions forever, or until the operator intervenes by deleting the program or pulling the plug out. See *Loop*.

Flowchart: A diagrammatic representation of the logical sequence of instructions in a program (see Chapter 12). A flowchart is supposed to be prepared by the programmer before getting down to the detailed step of writing out the instructions. (Often drawn afterwards because some programmers think they can write a good program without one.)

Testing: Running a program with sample data, in order to debug it.

Operating system: A special-purpose control program which is available to the machine all the time it is switched on. The operating system does many basic operations which were performed by hardware in older machines, or which are common to many programs. Referred to with such mystical terms as OS—for heaven's sake pronounce this as OH-ESS in the USA or Oss in the UK, or DOS; DE-OH-ESS in the USA or DOSS in the UK.

Finally, we can turn our attention to a general set of terms which will always stand you in good stead:

GIGO: Garbage in, garbage out. More elegantly, the quality of the computer output is limited by the quality of the input.

Data preparation: Abbreviated as data prep. Transcribing information into a form which can be read by a computer, such as punched cards or paper tape. Also used for the department which does this.

Punch operator (or key punch operator): Somebody who works in data prep.

I/O: Input/Output. Depending on the context, can mean input *and* output, or input *or* output.

And most important:

Black box: Any piece of equipment which only the engineers really understand.

Card, punched: What must not be folded, bent, or mutilated.

This is a basic set of jargon to start with. You will learn more as you read the book. If you really want to keep up-to-date, study the computer trade journals, conference reports, and specialized text books. You might even learn the new jargon before *they* do.

It should be made clear at this point, however, that we are *not* recommending that you actually talk this way. Knowing the jargon is your secret weapon; the computer people won't be able to dazzle you. For day-to-day work insist that they speak plain English when talking to you. The discipline is good for them; and it establishes them as servants of business, not masters—an important psychological point.

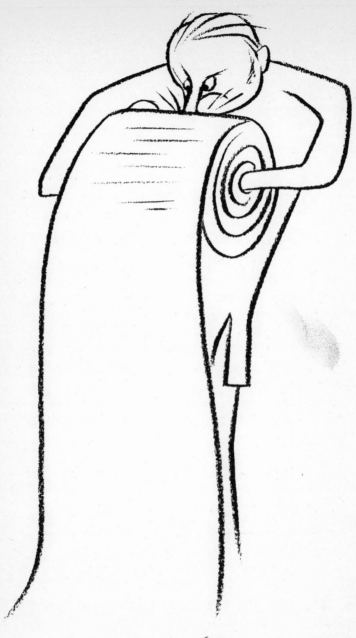

4

Why Not to Have a Computer

If your company already has a computer, you probably have your own views. You may know already that they shouldn't have got it, and why. You may still be making up your mind. Or you might support the decision (because you pushed the idea in the first place). In the first chapter we discussed the reasons for having a computer and gave some examples of the types of business which really benefit from one. But the fact remains that many companies which now have computers should have stuck to the old way of doing things, or rented time on someone else's, or got some other kind of special equipment instead—for example, accounting machines. Some companies which had small computers should not have changed to a bigger one: they could have improved efficiency on the small one to get more work out, or even bought another small one. Then, at least, they would have known what they were getting and what problems to anticipate.

Several years ago, we did a study for a large transport company. The recommendation was that they should *not* get a computer. But management over-ruled the report and decided to get one anyway—they were entranced by the salesman's claims. Recently we met one of the managers in a restaurant and got into a conversation with him. We asked about the computer. 'That thing,' he moaned. 'Never should have got it. Worst thing we ever did. It has been no end of trouble.'

A group of senior executives were at a seminar. One man worked for a group of companies that had been using computers for some time, and he was not very happy about it. Another executive was thinking about a computer. The disillusioned man passed on the benefit of his bitter experience to the neophyte. He produced statistics to show that in his group, 75 per cent of the computer projects had been failures—that is, as far as anyone could tell. And he said his company was typical. The other executive leapt to the defense of computers and his company's decision to get one. The first man looked gloomily at the other, perhaps with a touch of pity. 'And with all those failures,' he said, 'what makes you think your company is going to be any different?'

A very few companies have been brave enough to throw the computer out after realizing it's not for them. Going back to the old ways of working, however, can be as expensive as it was to put in computer systems, and in some cases it is impossible.

There are a few very good *general* reasons for not having a computer, and some reasons which apply only in special situations. We have two purposes for stating them: first, for those whose companies don't have a computer, as ammunition in the battle to stop it from happening, if you don't want one. And second, for those already stuck with one, this is the starting-point for keeping it under control. The next chapter will go further with specific suggestions for keeping it at bay.

THE FIRST LAW OF COMPUTER FAILURE

If the company has bad management, a computer will only make it worse. Or, at best, little will be achieved. A typical case is the company in which there is no planning and control, retrospective problem-solving (solving yesterday's problems today and to hell with tomorrow), and management by panic. The workers have a don't-care attitude. The political situation is so bad a manager spends 90 per cent of his time covering his rear. The last thing you need is better management information from a computer. You need new managers.

Another common situation is the company with poor management-worker relations. The two groups don't talk to each other, and the workers trust management like Tom trusts Jerry. A computer system is very risky in this climate. The present procedures are probably working only through inertia and luck; it would be disastrous to try to change them without solving the underlying problem.

A computer can alienate your staff

A few years ago you heard a lot about automation putting people out of work. The specter raised its head again during the last business recession, when many companies turned to the computer department to help cut costs; and sometimes even the computer people found themselves at the unemployment office. But those in the know realize that *the business computer, in the long run, creates more jobs than it destroys.* Think of the thousands who work for IBM and the other computer manufacturers. If you have a data-processing department, count the operators, programmers, key-punch girls etc. Further afield, look in the newspapers for all those advertisements for jobs in data processing; they provide work for newspaper people, employment agencies, and the company personnel department, just to mention a few. That computers create unemployment is a myth.

However, there has certainly been much dislocation because of computers. Some *jobs* may be eliminated, even if the people aren't. The nature of a man's job may change, his work may become less interesting. Departments are moved around, people become separated from their friends. In one company we worked in, management announced that no one would lose his job because of the computer. About thirty programmers were needed; every employee was given an aptitude test and those with good scores were offered jobs in the computer department. It meant more money and prestige, but some of those to whom new jobs were offered didn't accept; they didn't want to be separated from their friends. They liked the work they were doing and wanted to keep on doing it. This is perfectly understandable. A man is hired for a certain job and trained for it; why should he change willy-nilly?

Your best staff may leave, either to work in the computer department or to go to another company which still does things the old-fashioned way. They may be forced to retire early. If they stay, unless suitable preventive steps are taken, their jobs may become less interesting and there will certainly be considerable disruption. The data processing people may be arrogant and unsympathetic and cause bad feelings. Most businesses depend for their success on the loyalty and hard work of their staffs; why endanger this for the dubious advantages of having a computer?

You can't see your records any more

In the old days you had your files right there in your office, or at least next door. If you wanted to look up something, you walked over and opened the filing-cabinet, or you asked your secretary to do it for you. If a customer called up with an inquiry about his order or his account, you had instant access to the information. If you wanted to analyze sales of a certain product over the last two months, or check on outstanding invoices, you just got out the right files and papers.

With a computer none of this will be possible. All your records are stored on magnetic tapes and disk files. Even if you were allowed near them (and for safety reasons most companies rule that only the experts can handle the computer files), you couldn't read what was on them. If you bring this up with the systems analyst, he will chuckle indulgently and promise you a weekly print-out of everything on the files. Not only is this very expensive (guess who pays for it?), but also the data will be at least a week out of date by the time you get it, probably more.

There is another problem, too: what about errors on those

files? Perhaps the computer doesn't make mistakes, but the people feeding it can, and frequently do. When you handled the papers yourself, you could see that the customer's name was spelled wrong, you would know that the XYZ company never ordered that many widgets. The key-punch operators who prepare the data for the computer don't know this and don't care; the computer operators don't have time to look at it. The only possible answer is again for the computer to print out everything for your department to check. If you're doing all the work anyway, why have a computer?

Getting changes is difficult if not impossible

It is expensive and time-consuming to program the machine to do something a certain way. It's even more expensive and time-consuming to change it later. Suppose, for example, that you want a new report. Perhaps the nature of the business is changing, or you have some new products, or the department is growing, or there's a new law that you have to supply certain information to a government department. Whatever the reason, the information you need is there in the files. The computer has to be programmed, the programs have to be tested. Maybe the programmers are busy doing something else; they're paid a lot of money and can't sit around waiting for work. Extra computer time has to be found for testing, and it may not be reasonable to ask that the computer schedule be disrupted, inconveniencing everybody else, for this one report. It may be weeks before the new report is available; more likely it will take months. In some cases, unless you can convince the data processing department that you absolutely have to have it and can get top management to back you up, you may never get it at all.

If the change you are asking for is a very interesting one from the point of view of the systems people and programmers, if it's something new they haven't done before or represents a challenge, you are more likely to get it. But if it's just an ordinary, common or garden report you're probably out of luck. This kind of maintenance work on existing computer systems is considered to be dull and boring, and only the trainees or the programmers at the bottom of the pecking order in the data processing department will do it.

Let's do a comparison. You want a report of selected information from your manual records. Organizing it may be relatively simple: you get a group of clerks and tell them what to do, and you make certain they do it. Easy to set up, but with many records to go through it can take time. With a computer, the problems are reversed; it's harder to set up but quicker once you get started.

Computers are less flexible than people. Like the lack of visibility of records, the inflexibility of computer systems is a very real problem. It's a serious disadvantage of computers, for which there is no solution. Companies who are convinced they need a computer have to be prepared to put up with these disadvantages; one can only hope that the benefits more than outweigh the problems.

Confidential information is at risk

There are a number of reasons for this. First, the compactness of the data; it is possible to get the entire Encyclopedia Britannica on computer files that can be carried in one hand. Your entire department's files, on computer media, could fit into somebody's attache case.

Secondly, the fact that nobody can actually see the data any more. This may seem to be argument for better safety, but consider this: suppose there was a dishonest computer operator who had been tempted by an offer from your biggest competitor. They bribe him to get them a copy of your files. All he has to do is take a label off the reel of magnetic tape that has your file and put on a different one—perhaps the new label says 'Bad tape—to be cleaned'. Who's to prove differently when he walks out of the building with it? This has actually happened to more than one company.

A third reason for the greater risk is that your files are at a remote location; they're in a different department, perhaps even a different building. You no longer have control over them. If they're worth their pay, the computer people make copies of all important files and keep them outside the building in case of fire or other disaster. The original files may be safely under lock and key, but what about those copies? (If there aren't any copies, the computer manager should be drawn and quartered at dawn. Tomorrow.) With your old paper files, when they contained important or confidential information, you could lock the filing-cabinet yourself and take the key home with you. Now you are at the mercy of strangers who may not know or care which files have sensitive data on them.

You also have a responsibility to your customers and employees if the files contain any personal information. What right does the computer operator have to see details of medical records, loans or other financial information, personnel records? Or anybody else in the computer department, for that matter? Yet most of them probably have easy access to any files they may want to see; it's out of your control.

There is a solution to this problem, but it's an expensive one. The answer is a comprehensive security system in the data processing department, one that's *enforced* and kept up to date. But good security costs more when a computer is involved, for the reasons given above. It's apt to be neglected in the rush to get the computer systems working, and after a few years inertia sets in. We never had it before, why should we have it now? If good security is too expensive, then the computer is too expensive.*

The high technology cost spiral

If you work in the aerospace industry, electronics, or any research

* There is another point-of-view on computer security. The two executives at the seminar (the old hand and the innocent) were discussing these problems. The innocent extolled the various security techniques planned for his company. The old hand sighed. 'We can't get the information out of our damn machine even when we do want it. The crooks don't have a chance.'

and development department, you will know exactly what this means. It is a fact of modern life that if you invest in any high-technology based venture, you are likely to get your fingers burned. Development budgets and schedules are difficult to set and harder to meet. Exceeded estimates are the rule. It is difficult to think of any major high-technology development project which has not run over budget and been delayed. If you're in the high-technology area, you know this; we know it; but the businessman in an ordinary commercial company only knows about IBM typewriters and Xerox machines. In the high-technology area, which includes any computer project, *everything costs more and takes longer*.

Mistakes are magnified

Incorrect data can get into the computer system just as it gets into ordinary paper files. The programs may have undetected bugs in them, and the processing is being done incorrectly. A computer does everything faster, including processing incorrect data; there may be just as many errors as in the old system, except that now they're happening faster, cost more, and take longer to find and correct. You might as well stay with the old system; at least they're *your* mistakes and you can find them and fix them without going broke.

There are some things people do better

We have an imaginary character we call 'Bob Smith'. He is the transport manager who organizes deliveries with a fleet of twenty-five trucks. He never writes anything down, but he can tell you exactly where each truck is at any moment. You can't plan the deliveries with a computer better than he can. What happens when a truck breaks down? A parade causes traffic jams? Road works mean a new route has to be chosen on the spot? Bob Smith gets reports from his drivers all day long. He knows what to do.

   Bob Smith is also a seventy-year-old buyer in a shoe company.

Can a computer predict next year's fashions? Not better than Bob Smith can. He can't explain *how* he does it, but he does.

Or Bob Smith is an editor with an unerring nose for next year's best-seller, a warehouseman who knows exactly how many boxes will fit into a given space, by sizing it by eye; a sales manager with forty years of experience he can't articulate.

Don't replace your Bob Smiths with a computer. You may have to when they die or retire, but it can only be to your loss.

BAD REASONS FOR HAVING A COMPUTER

No discussion of why not to have a computer would be complete without a list of some of the *wrong* reasons for having one. Few companies buy a computer for purely rational reasons, human nature being what it is. One or more of the following may be an unwritten reason why management has talked themselves into the decision: 'Yes, we'll get one.'

1. Everybody else has one. This is the ultimate in keeping up with the Joneses.

2. To improve the company image. Especially if the chairman's golf buddies all work for companies with computers.

3. To prevent a merger or takeover. With a computer, everything is such a mess the company can't possibly be absorbed into another one.

4. Profits are good. Why give the money to the taxman or the shareholders when you can waste it on a computer?

5. Because nothing else has worked. The company has so many problems it is hoped a computer will be the universal answer. Of course it isn't; the problems just get worse.

6. To clear out the dead wood. For example, to get rid of elderly executives. They know nothing about computers, and so are forced into early retirement.

7. As a power base. He who controls the computer controls the company. Power-hungry senior managers can use the computer to increase their influence.

8. To act out a fantasy. Computer salesmen don't sell computers; they sell the future.

9. As a smokescreen. The computer directs attention away from other things management is doing at the same time, like reorganizing the company or losing money. The computer can be blamed for everything.

10. If it is technically feasible, it is desirable. This is the technicians' argument.

11. Because no one can think of good reasons *not* to have a computer. (They obviously haven't read this chapter.) This is the technological snowball effect; we have typewriters so we might as well have accounting machines; we have accounting machines, so we should move up to punched card tabulators; and from punched cards, a computer is the next logical step.

5

How Not to Have a Computer

We are now at the point where one of two situations exists. Either the company doesn't have a computer, but certain people are beginning to talk about getting one; or a computer is already installed, and you're afraid that your department is on the list to get a computer system. Either way you want to block any further so-called 'progress'. There is a third possibility, which is that you've already got a computer system. Many of the suggestions below can be modified to help you get rid of it, or at the very least prevent any more expansion of the computer's sphere of influence—no small victory in itself.

Remember there are people whose livelihood depends on computers. You will have to be prepared for them. A computer salesman's job for example, is to counter the anti-computer people.

We went out for a quiet meal the other night. Henri showed us to a secluded table, but, to our surprise, it proved to be a sound trap for the table opposite, occupied by a senior company executive and a senior salesman from a very large and powerful computer company. Making frantic notes on the back of the menu, we analyzed his approach:

Opening gambit: Praise to the executive for working for a progressive company; progressive because they are thinking about a computer, and even more progressive because it's one of his.

No response

Second gambit: The computer is 'upwards compatible'. This means the computer can grow to keep pace with the dynamic growth of the company . . . due, of course, to the computer.

No response

Third: Computer will give better management information, invaluable to a growing company, as many of its competitors have discovered.

Slight response

Fourth: And, of course, he (the executive) would be responsible for the successes of the new computer venture, gain more power and influence, and so on.

Negative response

Final ploy: My boss knows your boss, so play ball, buddy.

The higher up in management you are, the more likely you will be able to exert authority, and the better your chances of preventing the purchase of a computer. But there are some tactics even the lowliest can employ with success. Study the suggestions below carefully, and pick out the ones that will work best in your particular situation. Modify and embellish them at will to suit individual circumstances.

Spend the money on something else

This can work only if you are in a high enough position to authorize large expenditures; or, possibly, if you can requisition a new warehouse and get it. There will then be no money in the kitty for a computer, and its acquisition has to be postponed until next year. Next year, you think of something else the company needs more urgently than a computer. This will work indefinitely, or until the company is bankrupt.

Get a committee to study the proposal

This delaying tactic has been used for centuries, and still works beautifully. If possible, get people for the committee who have so many other problems they never have time to meet. Urge them to take their time over such an important decision. Make the committee as large as possible; remember Parkinson's law on this, that once a committee has more than twenty-one members, people have to stand up to be heard; and once on their feet a speech is inevitable; nothing will ever get done. If it looks as if they might actually agree on something, add a new member. They will then have to go back to the beginning and start over again.*

Praise it to death

Sing the hymn of computers long and loud, at every opportunity. People will soon get so sick of hearing you they won't even want to think about computers. (We know one manager who tried this but failed. His crusading did, however, pay off; he is now—unkindest cut of all—the data processing manager.)

Find out how much it will really cost

From the experience of others, the cost will be at least twice as much as it seemed at first, sometimes three times as much. Demand a more *detailed* study to work out the true cost. This in itself will delay everything six months. When the pro-computer people give you the figure, first look to see if it's a round number. $800,000.00 can't be right, it's not detailed enough. Send them back to do it again. If it's $834,693.26, quibble over the 26c—if you can show they're off by a few cents, the whole figure is in doubt, and you can send them back to do it again.

* You might get Parkinson's committee size to work for you, but remember you'll have his Law of Triviality working *against* you: 'The time spent on any item on the agenda will be in inverse proportion to the sum involved.' A computer budget of half a million might get through in ten minutes flat if you're not careful. If the Law of Triviality looks like applying, immediately point out that the computer means more coat racks for the extra people at a cost of $11.30 each. And, don't let them focus on the total budget figure, but make them consider each item: desks for programmers, pencils, coding pads, and so on.

Get lots of manufacturers to bid

There are at least six American computer manufacturers with similar machines, and a number of English ones. After that, try the French and the Japanese; they're coming up fast in the computer market. Every one will have to come into the company to make a study, then recommend the right computer for you with all the optional extras. This takes time. There is a further advantage that they will get in everyone's hair and make the idea of a computer seem less and less attractive every day. Only *one* computer salesman will convince them; six or eight in a row, ending with an inscrutable Oriental or two, will have them climbing the walls. *Then* you set up a committee to evaluate all the proposals. This tactic is good for at least two years of delay, more if you really try.

Keep changing the specifications

This works equally well in delaying the computer itself, or delaying a computer system. Wait until all the details have been worked out, but before an order has been placed or programming begun. Then change your mind about what you want. If you have been using other delaying tactics successfully, the changes could be quite legitimate; every business evolves over a period of years—there may be new legal requirements, new products, and so on. Don't tell them about all the changes at once, hold back a few for later.

Hire a consultant

Insist that what is needed is an objective, outside opinion. You can spend six months just choosing the consultant. He will take another six months to prepare a report. If you are the one who authorizes payment of his fee, make sure he knows what you want the recommendation to be.

Demand the impossible

Ask for something which is too expensive, or better yet, technologically beyond the state of the art at the moment. Chapter 18 may give you some ideas. A full-scale data base, for example, can take ten years just for the initial study.

Change your present method of working

This is a very elegant ploy, and has numerous advantages. First, absolutely nothing can be done about a new computer system while you are in the middle of the change; they have to wait until the details are finalized. If a computer project is already under way, all the work up to now will have to be scrapped. By the time the changes are completed, you can claim a) that the problems are now solved and a computer is unnecessary, and b) that you have spent so much money on the change that nothing is left for the computer.

The best kind of change involves a complete reorganization of the department, or the whole company if you can manage it, with a lot of job-shuffling. Then the erstwhile computer people can be eased out of positions of influence, and nobody even knows who to talk to.

Overwhelm them with jargon

Turn the computer people's best weapon against them. Don't try to beat them at their own game with *computer* jargon—they can make it up faster than you can learn it; just use the ordinary business jargon you always use. Every business has its own vocabulary. Insurance is a particularly good example; they've been devising their own special words for two thousand years. Bear down heavily on confusing business terms, and be vague when asked for explanations. If they can't understand what you do, they can't put it on the computer.

47

Hide behind the union

If your employees are in a union, this is sure-fire. Tell the computer people that you don't want to rock the boat of management-union relations. If management has a good relationship with the union, say you don't want to endanger it. If it's bad, why, talking about a computer would only make it worse and might cause a strike. A refinement on this technique is to use Catch 22: no computer system can be put in without the union's approval, but nobody can talk to them about it.

Make them prove their success

This tactic, and the next, assume that the computer has been installed for some time, and many other departments have systems running. Before they can go ahead with yours, make them prove the others were successful. It is extremely unlikely that they'll be able to because a) they never knew what they were doing in the first place, and b) even if they did, no one has had time to evaluate the results.

Use the computer department history against them

This is the easiest one of all in a company which has had a computer for a while. They are certain to have made botch-ups and have had disasters. If your company is typical, the data-processing people are universally disliked and mistrusted. All you have to do is to keep reminding everybody including them, of all their past sins. You have the best reason in the world for not letting them get their grubby little hands on your department.

If all these tactics fail, then the rest of the book is written for you. If you succeed in blocking the computer, you will really enjoy reading the rest of the book to see what you're missing.

6

So You've Got a Computer Anyway

We are assuming now that your company has a computer and your work, voluntarily or otherwise on your part, is going on the computer.

In the beginning . . .

If you have not yet been involved in a computer system, you may be wondering how it begins. In this example, we will assume that you are a personnel manager, although it doesn't really matter who you are. You are responsible for various functions, including industrial relations, salary administration, recruitment, and staff welfare. You are also responsible for the monthly and weekly payrolls. It is the latter area to which we will confine our discussion. There is a section that receives details of new employees and leavers, details of time worked etc. You maintain payroll records of each employee, and at the appropriate time prepare the pay information and arrange for the accounts department to make the actual payments.

This work must be done. You are happy with the way it's working. People are being paid the correct amount on time and it is costing about 15c each. Eighteen months later, a computer is being used to process the payroll. What happened? Why should this come about? There are many reasons:

Because it's there: A very common reason, based on almost irrefutable logic. The company has a computer. There is a spare time-slot. Computers are good at doing basic record-keeping. Let's computerize the payroll. We've filled the time-slot, and the computer people have had something to do.

We can do it better: This is the computer manager telling you that computers are ideal for running the payroll and will do it better than the present system. We'll get the cost per payslip down, and give you lots of statistical reports.

You decide you can do it better on the computer: This is almost the same as the last, but here you are sealing your own fate. You know that half a dozen companies in the neighborhood are doing payroll on the computer and they can't all be wrong, can they?*

The same thing happened in each of these situations. *You and them never decided what you wanted to achieve.* The solution came first: put it on the computer. This may have solved some problems (if only you could think of them now), but it's certainly generated some.

Other ways computer systems get started are:

The wider scope of things: Most invidious. Management decides that the company will introduce a sophisticated integrated systems approach. This means they can see that all the information in the company is inter-related in some way. They are right, of course. To produce cost of sales, or cost of production, they will need to incorporate labor costs. Labor costs come from your payroll system. Production control (in another division) is being put on the computer. Therefore, to get detailed costs of production, the payroll system must be computerized as well.

Help! If 'the wider scope' is invidious, 'help' is the saddest, because *you tried*. Things haven't been quite right with the payroll. You have problems with rising costs, lateness, accuracy. You called for help from the management services department; as it turned out, this was a cunning disguise for the computer department. And the computer department took over. They gave you

* They can.

a computer system. But naturally, while they were doing that, they took the chance to solve other problems (which you never knew you had) in personnel records, manpower-planning, revision of salary structures, and so on.

This can be a stepping-stone for even further computerization. Having computerized the payroll, it makes sense to computerize production costing, thereby producing computerized production control. And there you are; *they* are running the company.

Let's look at the way computer projects *should* go.

ELEVEN STEPS

Developing and implementing a computer-based system can be a major project. Obviously, the scope of the project determines the amount of work and the amount of time involved. There's a big difference, for example, between putting a small local payroll on the computer and installing a company-wide personnel records system. Most companies go through steps like those listed below. These eleven steps start with selecting the application for computerization and go on to operational running of the new system. Some companies call these steps by other names, or compress two or three steps into one. They will be described in more detail throughout the book.

1 *User request or exploratory study*

This involves defining the business problem(s), the starting-point which can determine the success or failure of the project. It includes a statement of objectives (what the system has to achieve), boundaries and constraints (what the system mustn't do and the area of the company where the solution is required), time-scale (when the system is required). No mention of a computer yet. This is the time when *you* should define what is wanted from the business point of view. The solution, *possibly* a computer-based system, comes in the next step, the feasibility study.

The user request has to be considered with all the other user's requirements: what priority should your project have and how will your project overlap with others? Most large companies have a long-term plan and policy for computers. Your project must be slotted in or matched against this plan.

Let's say, for example, that you work in an insurance company, and a new type of insurance is being brought out. It seems logical to have a computer system for it, so you put in a user request. There are already other departments with requests in. Do you have to go to the end of the line and wait your turn? The question can only be answered by looking at your project in relation to the others. On the one hand, it would seem silly—not to say expensive —for you to have to hire and train a team of clerks to process the new work for only six months or a year. On the other hand, someone else's problems may be costing the company even more, and they deserve priority.

The user request is discussed in detail in Chapter 7.

2 *Feasibility study*

You've stated what you want to achieve in business terms; you may also have defined the problems that are preventing you from meeting your business targets or objectives. The feasibility study looks for a solution. It presents an outline solution (or solutions), at least one with a computer system. It will show the cost of developing and running the system and the benefits of it. The study should give a sense of direction for further development work; it doesn't give a solution in depth. The details could be expensive to work out and this expense should not be incurred until you have approved the basic idea and the way that the project will be tackled. (The feasibility study step is described in Chapter 8.)

3 *Investigation*

You have accepted the findings and recommendations of the feasibility study and given the go-ahead to develop the system.

The first step will be a detailed investigation of the existing environment: the people their jobs, the organization, the data, the procedures, and the future information requirements. This is aimed at expanding the findings of the review which took place during the feasibility study, and will be used as the basis for subsequent analysis and design. Any new system must fit in with the existing environment, or specific recommendations must be made as to how the environment must be changed. If this step is missed, the new system has little chance of working. (See Chapter 10.)

4 *Analysis*

The mass of information collected during investigation is organized, sifted and reviewed. The analyst determines what the new system must do, the problems to be solved, and the data, people, and procedures which form the basis of the existing environment.

5 *Design*

From analysis, the analyst knows what must be done in the new system and the problems to be solved. That is the design brief; his job now is to design the best possible system which does all the tasks and solves all the problems, thereby producing a solution which meets the requirements initially specified and agreed in the user request. The system design will cover all aspects of the new system: the data, the management and clerical procedures, the machine procedures (the programs), how the system will be tested and implemented. There is then a major checkpoint in which everybody approves the system, including the users. This is the last review point before the expensive tasks of programming, testing, and implementation begin. If you change the specification of the new system after this point, costs will rocket.

6 *Programming*

Part of the system design job is specifying, in outline, the computer processing requirements: what the computer must do. Each of the computer procedures will require a program to be written. Programming should not involve the user. It is a technical job of getting the computer part of the system to work.

7 Testing

During programming, each of the programs will be proved against the specifications provided and agreed by the analyst. The next task will be testing the whole system, including not only the computer processing but all the other manual procedures. You will become involved in supplying test data and reviewing the results.

8 Documentation

We are showing this as a separate step, but it is a continuing process all through systems development. The results of each phase of the development work are recorded. For example, how the system works as a whole, what the programs do and how they work, the manual procedures for getting information into the computer, dealing with the output from the computer, and so on. It is a vital task. You can only approve the system if it is documented; you and the computer people can only run the system if procedures are specified, and the system can only be maintained if the working of the system is clearly mapped out.

9 Conversion and implementation

This includes all the tasks of arranging for the new system to be installed and the actual changeover from the existing system. It covers training, getting new documents printed and issued for use, capturing work in progress, and setting up all the computer-based files so that live running can begin. In large clerical systems, this can be the most time-consuming, expensive, and frustrating task of the whole project. And who carries the brunt of the work? Yes, you do—or you ought to.

10 *Maintenance*

No business or business environment is static. As the business and its needs change, so the computer system must change to keep pace. Maintenance is the modification of a running system so that it matches the changes in the business.

11 *Evaluation*

We mention this step here, but in practice it is rarely done. This is a review of the system after it has been in operation for some time. It seeks to answer the questions: has the system achieved what was specified in the user request? Have we achieved it well, were the budgets and time-scales met? Have the requirements altered since the project started?

So this is an indication of the type and amount of work that you will be letting yourself in for if you get involved in a computer-based system. Many of these tasks will be described in greater detail later. There are, however, some things you should think about before embarking on a computer project.

Involvement

'Get involved' is the cry from many an enlightened data processing manager. If you want a computer system that really achieves something and a system that works, you must play your part. When the system is running, you and your staff will have to live with it. If you opt out during its development, or are excluded by the data processing department, the system will never be *your* system, but their system. It will work effectively only as long as the data processing department is propping it up; if any of your staff have problems with the system, they will go to the systems analyst, not you. The computer people generally dislike this as much as you would. We have seen more systems go sour during

57

development and after for this reason than for any other. This book will show you where your involvement is vital. If you choose for your own reasons to opt out, the system will probably be useless, at least to your department.

Checkpoints

These are formal review steps which take place at key points: after the feasibility study, after systems design, and so on. Work does not commence on the next step until the work on the previous one is complete *and approved*. It's a way for you to become involved at the right time, and it attempts to make certain that the data processing people don't waste their time and your money.

Planning

This means that you know when you and your people have to put in special effort during the systems development project. There is nothing more irksome than a phone call just before lunch asking you to have a complete set of 1,000 sample records ready for systems testing after lunch. It means that you and the data processing department will have to sit down and agree upon who does what, when, and how.

With this overview of the key tasks in developing a system, we can look at the individual steps in detail in chapters that follow.

7

Deciding What You Want and Getting It

If you want a computer system which is worthwhile, the most valuable contribution you can make is to *define the objectives for the system*. And this rests on one important assumption: *that you have business objectives set for your area of the company*. You can't manage, make rational decisions, organize your people, or make a computer system work, if you don't know what you're trying to achieve.

> *OBJECTIVES*—short-, medium-, and long-term
> *ENVIRONMENT*—your resources:
> — people and their jobs
> — procedures
> — organization
> — plant
> — raw material and stocks
> — money
> — information

Information is as much a resource as people and plant. Your task as a manager is to organize the environment so the objectives can be met: it's straight common-sense. If you don't have objectives, then how can you go about organizing your environment?

A computer-based system is just another way to organize, operate, and control the environment. Yet, there *are* differences between reorganizing the jobs that your people do and putting in a computer system: the computer system will cost more, take longer, and be far less flexible.

This is, of course, an over-simplified approach to the manager's role and his part in initiating a computer project. Your short- and medium-term objectives, for example, will be continually refined as the business requirements change and policy set from above is revised. There will be other stimuli too. One such may be the data processing manager who tells you he can cut your costs and make better use of resources; another is that the objectives of different parts of the company must be complimentary, so that the company is pulling together. Sometimes conflicting objectives can tear the company apart, and the computer can be a powerful aid in encouraging this. For example, in one large engineering company there were two major power-bases: production and marketing. The objectives of production were to standardize production methods, which meant cutting down drastically on modifications for special customer orders. Marketing, on the other hand, was trying to boost sales by any means. The way they were meeting this objective was to take *all* jobs, big and small, standard or special. A state of near civil war existed.

Another complication occurs when you are constrained from meeting objectives because of shortcomings elsewhere. For example, you are responsible for Department X and the basic information you need to operate comes from Department Y. If you get this information, you can do the job. It is here that senior management play their role in co-ordination and overall control.

Even if you have realistic, tactical objectives, you may not be able to meet them. If you can point to what is stopping you, you have identified the problems. The setting of objectives and match-ing environment against them is a continual process, and is a part of everyday management. If you don't have time to set and review objectives, or do basic reviews of progress against them, *you don't need a computer systems analyst—you need a management consultant.* Or the company needs a new manager.

So the starting-point of any computer project is setting business objectives. Without this, you will be investing a large sum of money without any purpose.

A set of objectives we found in one company was: 'The company is subject to a possible take-over, with a merger of production facilities with another company. Our objective is to stay independent. Therefore, we will computerize production.' The computerized mess could not be unravelled economically, and hence the merger would not be viable. The objectives were met.

Objectives should be quantified wherever possible. Rather than 'increase vehicle utilization', 'increase vehicle utilization by at least 5 per cent'. Not 'decrease order turn-around time', but 'decrease order turn-around to at least twelve hours'. For 'reduce inventory', 'reduce investment in inventory by 15 per cent'. There are occasions when setting formalized quantified objectives is difficult, sometimes impossible, as we will see in the next chapter. If so, a computer is largely an act of faith committed by management.

THE USER REQUEST

At the start of a computer project, define what you want, formally, in a document called the user request. This is the statement of the problem. You may do it by yourself, or with assistance. Many large companies are using 'business analysts' to help. If you are given a computer systems analyst to help you, then beware of being sidetracked onto computer solutions too early. One of the advantages of the user request is that it gives you the opportunity and initiative to specify what you want. Some notes on the contents are given below.

Objectives: A list of *all* the objectives, showing priority, quantified wherever possible.

Constraints: What the new system solution must *not* do. The constraints may be budgetary—you cannot afford more than so many dollars in the next fiscal year; or the system mustn't require the use of any more clerical staff because they just aren't available in the area.

Boundaries: This is an attempt to limit the scope of the project. You may be happy with the way part of the department works, or you have already made changes which you don't want to revoke. (If you're not careful, the computer people will attempt to get the widest possible brief, starting their review at one side of the company and working through to the other.)

Time-scale: When the solution is required. Not 'yesterday', but a time-scale with a business justification. For example, the new system may be required to coincide with the start of a new fiscal year, or stocktaking, or the introduction of a new product range. If you've left the request too late and are in a panic, it's not fair to expect the computer department to cover your own short-comings.

The computer people can then look for a solution. During the feasibility study, the computer systems analyst will, rightly, comment on the objectives, boundaries, constraints, and time-scales as he sees them. This is covered in the next chapter.

Finally, you're not the only one in the company with problems. All companies should have a long-term plan and policy for computer usage. Computer resources are restricted, and priorities have to be set on requests. Somebody must make sure that the requests are compatible. That means that all user requests must be checked out and approved by senior management; this is discussed in Chapter 24, 'The View from the Top'.

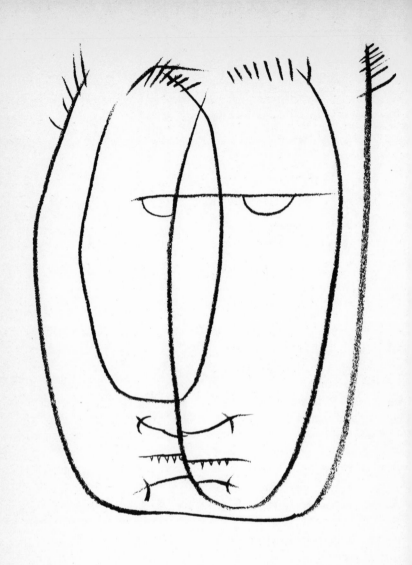

8

Lies, Damned Lies and Feasibility Studies

In the last chapter we discussed the formal user request, the basic statement of the problem. The objective of a feasibility study is to check the adequacy of the user request to find and outline solutions and to cost them. The important word here is *outline*; the study is aimed at giving a sense of direction so management can decide the future course of action. This is a risk venture, so a detailed system design is not practical now.

The feasibility study is based on an initial survey or investigation of the existing environment and future information requirements. A number of alternative systems are put forward and compared, so that the user can make a choice. There are two advantages to this approach. The first is that there may be more than one way of killing the cat, not necessarily a computer-based system. The second is that the user makes the choice; a decision entered into freely, a commitment. This is to everyone's advantage.

The range of possible solutions is:

— do nothing (no change)
— revise the manual system
— use limited automated facilities (accounting machines etc)

— use special problem-solving techniques, such as work
    study or operations research
— put in a small-scale, limited computer system
— put in a large-scale computer system

The first suggestion should appear in every study; it shows the
magnitude of the problems. Obviously, not all of the other
alternatives would apply in a given situation.

In a feasibility study, each alternative is described; what the
system is, how it would be developed and implemented, and
what it would achieve. This gives two sides of an equation:

COSTS   BENEFITS

The difference between the two is *savings* (or, of course,
losses). There will also be 'advantages and disadvantages' which
cannot be quantified in money terms. The costs will break down
into development, implementation, and running costs. The
benefits are implicit in the objectives: 'What is the benefit of
reducing inventory by 15 per cent?' 'What is the benefit of holding
personnel costs level over five years?', and so on.

Damned lies: benefits

No decent systems analyst is going to tell you outright lies. But
there can be ommissions, confusions, and ambiguities in the way
the report is presented and in the way you interpret it.

One can only determine benefits if the objectives are clearly
stated. In a well-organized project, the benefits have been worked
out before the feasibility study takes place. In many respects
the user is the best person to judge these. The analyst estimates
how well an objective is met by a particular solution and appor-
tions part of the benefit to it. The hardest part of the study is to
reconcile the differences between tangible and intangible benefits.
A schoolboy said to his father, 'Daddy, daddy, I ran home behind
a bus today and saved 20c.' 'Very good, son. Tomorrow run home
behind a taxi and save $5.' Where does a feasibility study end and
fantasy begin?

68

Most companies have three kinds of systems:

Record-keeping systems are the basis of all business information—these are systems which simply record details of events which have taken place. Examples are payroll, purchase ledger, sales ledger and stock-recording. The control systems operate on information from the record-keeping systems. A control system is concerned with making the best uses of the resources in the company. For example, with a sales ledger you can do credit control, debtor control, and sales forecasting. With a stock ledger and sales forecasting you can do inventory control.

The MIS (management information system) uses extracts and distillations from the mass of information in the record-keeping and control systems. A computer could be used in all three types of system. The criteria for usage will be something like:

'Better . . . at less cost or the same cost.'

Insert phrases like

— accurate information
— faster and more timely information
— information of the right scope

There are two basic rules in assessing the benefits of an information-processing system:

1. The higher up the information hierarchy you are, the greater the potential benefits but the less certainty there is of achieving them.

2. You can't have a successful computer-based control or MIS system unless it's built on a sound record-keeping base.

For example, if stock-recording were computerized, the potential savings in the computerized record-keeping system may be 'saving' two or three clerks. With careful planning you can be pretty certain that these small benefits will be realized. A system at a higher level, like inventory control, can have a far greater potential benefit for the company. But whether you attain the benefit will be far less certain.

Below are some basic rules for the proposed benefits of a new computer system.

The 'so what?' test: A phrase beloved of computer systems analysts and salesmen is '. . . and the system will efficiently produce management information not currently available in the existing system'. If you receive a proposal which lists various management reports, review each report and ask yourself, 'So what?' For example, you are offered a sales statistics report showing sales by product each month, compared to this month last year. So what? Do you want this information, all of it? What do you use it for? Ah, you want to see what products are doing well and what ones are doing badly. Then why not get a report showing *just* those (you set the criteria for good and bad) and skip that bulky report where most of the products are doing OK and don't need looking at. *Information should not be produced as a product in its own right. It must meet a business need.*

Mixed benefits: Never give benefits equal weight if they have different degrees of certainty associated with them. For example, in an order-processing system:

— The new system takes away clerical work from salesmen, leaving them more time to sell. The present amount of time spent on clerical work is 15 per cent, reduced in the new system to 5 per cent, leaving 10 per cent more time

to sell. If sales are $2 million, the benefit is $200,000.
— Staff saving in stock control will be two clerks @ $10,000
   per year including overheads, for a saving of $20,000.
— Total benefit: $220,000.

Oh yes? The probability of achieving those benefits is entirely
different. In a case like the first, apply the 'what if' test. What if
the salesmen merely take a longer lunch-hour or cut down on
overtime? What if the market is already saturated using current
sales techniques? The probability of realizing the total benefit is
less than in the second case.

Ideally, the benefit figures should be shown on different pages
something like this:

Page 1: Definite benefits.
Page 2: Probables, with a list of assumptions and
         provisos.
Page 3: Might happen (and good-oh if they do).

Act of faith: Every attempt must be made to quantify the benefits.
Only after this is done should you be faced with a decision based on
faith. It might even be a hunch. For example, the new system will
set up and maintain scientific and technical abstracts related to
your work. It is aimed at getting the right paper to the right
researcher at the right time. The possible benefits are twofold.
One is cutting down the time spent by research technicians'
searching abstracts. So what? Will the time saved be spent on
more useful areas of work? Second, by getting the right paper to
the right man at the right time, the quality of research will be
improved. Perhaps a scientific breakthrough takes place. This is
where faith comes in. You can't quantify the benefits and you
can't put any odds on the probabilities.

Too much too quickly: This can be a logical failure in calculating
the benefits. It takes time for a computer-based system to pick
up steam. If the feasibility report shows the button being pushed
and, presto, benefits come out, someone is fooling himself. It
just doesn't work that way. Suppose the analyst proposes a system

to be installed in two phases, and the feasibility study shows 100 per cent of the benefits realized with phase one only, in the first year. So much for phase two.

Lies: costs

You are more in the hands of the systems analyst when it comes to costs. He's the expert. To arrive at the development and running costs, he must have an outline of the new system and plans for developing and implementing it. Remember that costing is a cyclical process; first estimates are refined as the project progresses, with more reliable figures produced. But if the costs increase by 20 per cent or more every time they are revised, something was wrong with the plans in the first place.

Some common costing errors are:

Omissions: Not including *all* the costs. When you look at estimated development costs, see if the time and effort of non-computer people is included, including those in your own department. Also, see if an allowance has been made for maintaining the system after it is installed (see Chapter 15).

Forgetting intangible costs: For example, the cost of disruption caused by changing over to the new system; the business you can't do because your people are spending time helping the computer department.

The take - care - of - the - dollars - and - pennies - will - take - care - of - themselves attitude: If the biggest single cost—programming—is $150,000, who worries about a few thousand dollars for extras? The feasibility study is a contract between the user and data processing; contracts must have detail. Those odd thousands of dollars add up fast.

Too complicated: Remember Heller's Seventh Law of Management: 'If you need sophisticated calculations to justify an action, it is probably wrong.' In one company we know of the computer users took this to heart. They didn't understand how the computer time was being charged to them and they went on strike, refusing to authorize any new systems.

By all means use NPV (Net Present Value) or DCF (Discounted Cash Flow) on the cost figures, but don't let the systems analyst try and re-try until he finds a combination that justifies the system.

When the feasibility study is finished, the user is responsible for studying it and then for deciding which of the alternatives he wants. For the purposes of the rest of this book, we assume that some form of computer system has been chosen.

9

When the Systems Analyst Visits You

When the computer project is underway, sooner or later someone from the computer department, probably a systems analyst, will come to talk to you. In fact, if you don't receive a visit, it probably means the analyst is designing a system *he* thinks you ought to have, and it won't be the one *you* actually need.

If you are against the project you may postpone the evil day by taking a vacation, pretending you're sick, or saying you're too busy. But if the analyst is any good, he'll get to see you in the end.

First of all, the type of person he is likely to be. He'll probably be young and not know very much about business and management in general or your business in particular. (It comes as a great surprise to some analysts to find that the company is actually in business to make money.) Chances are he's a promoted programmer; he may have been a very good programmer, but that doesn't necessarily mean he's a good systems analyst.

Secondly, why does he come to see you? The first step in developing a computer-based system will be an investigation. A general investigation will take place (or should) when a computer system is first considered, that is, at the feasibility study stage. A more detailed investigation is done when the project is underway. This in-depth fact-finding concerns all aspects of the business: the people, the jobs, the organization, the procedures, the data. A computer system is far less flexible than its clerical counterpart. To program the computer, all the actions to be taken must be specified in detail. This means that every item of data must be very carefully considered. Suppose you use a code to identify your products. To use the product code on the computer, the designer must know:

— how is the code allocated?
— who allocates a new code or deletes an old one?
— when are the codes allocated and dropped?
— how many codes now and in the future?
— what is the pattern of codes in use—are there gaps or clusters in the sequence?
— what is the composition of the code—how long is it (number of characters), how is it made up (alphabetics, numbers, special symbols)?
— who uses the code and why?

You may have lived with the product code system for years and know it thoroughly; the analyst won't, and that's why he comes to see you. In fact, you might know only some of the answers yourself because:

— you're too high up in the organization to worry about such mundane matters of detail, or
— you're too low down in the organization to see the whole picture.

The analyst needs to see the system as a whole; so he visits many people, fitting together the answers like a giant jig-saw puzzle.

What happens if he doesn't pick up all the pieces, or loses some of them, or gets them in the wrong shape? The system won't work. When it's designed, it must fit into your current method of working, or you must know specifically what you will have to change. If a system is designed and then just superimposed on your present working methods, there will be trouble. Reports which keep the department working aren't produced, the input forms are far too complex to fill in, special circumstances aren't catered for and cause chaos when they occur. The quality of the design of the system rests upon the quality of the analysis, and that rests on the completeness and accuracy of the investigation:

So the investigation is the very important starting-point. If it is done well, your problems still aren't over; you have to make certain that the results of the investigation are in fact used in analysis and design, not just tucked away in a filing-cabinet to gather dust.

We will ask the questions . . .

If you have never come into contact with an analyst before and are a bit nervous, the following four rules will help you.

Rule 1: Don't be afraid of him. If he doesn't know you, he's probably more frightened of you than you are of him. (If he isn't, then he should be; hold onto that thought.)

Rule 2: Never forget that you know more about your job than he does, or is ever likely to. Don't let him fool you. Also remember that you and others like you in the company have, by dint of your own efforts, made the company profitable enough to be able to afford a computer and the systems analysts to go with it. Indirectly, you pay his salary. Hold onto that thought as well.

Rule 3: Don't let him waste your time. Investigation isn't just

77

wandering around the company, asking questions here and there. When he comes to see you, he should have a list of questions prepared or a summary of topics to be discussed. And he should write down the answers. If he doesn't, the interview will turn into an aimless chat and he'll remember little or nothing of what you tell him. One of three things will then happen:

— the interview will take five times as long as it should.
— he'll have to come back over and over again to ask the same questions.
— he'll mis-remember what you said and his recommendations will bear little or no resemblance to what you really want and need.

He's wasted your time. The truly professional analyst will go into investigation with the objective of:

Getting the maximum of right information in the minimum of time, while performing a 'PR' function (being diplomatic, showing you that the computer department knows what it's doing, and at the same time leaving you with the impression that you've had a fair hearing).

The only way to achieve this is to go about the investigation in a logical way, preparing each step in advance. *So if he hasn't prepared, or if he doesn't take notes of your answers, throw him out.* Tell him to come back when he's prepared, and not before.

If he relies on *observation*, be careful. If he says that the main way to investigate a system is to do the job, he's not only naive but dangerous. Of course the analyst will need to temper his interviews with a look at what happens in practice.

If he grabs at a procedure manual, organization chart, or job description and says, 'I won't need to take any more of your time; these will answer my questions', then he is more than naive and dangerous; he's downright stupid. And you are compounding his folly if you don't stop him. Except in a few military installations, these documents do not define all eventualities, are not up-to-date, or don't reflect the informal hierarchies and methods of working. They might make good *background* reading—but that's all.

If he uses a questionnaire, be careful. It should be thought of as a last resort, when people are too scattered to interview. Preparing a questionnaire is a difficult and specialized job. Even with the best thought-out ones, a certain amount of back-up work needs to be done. So don't waste your time filling in half-baked questionnaires; get on the phone and ask what the hell he wants to know and why.

Rule 4: *If you are a manager, make certain the analyst checks with you before seeing the people under you.* They will want to know:

— 'what's it all about?'
— 'where will I stand when the computer goes in?'
— 'will I lose my job?'
— 'has someone been complaining about the way I do my job?'

The analyst has to answer these questions in one way or another. If you want to avoid strikes, despondency, sabotage, and other disorders, brief the analyst on how you want the questions dealt with. Better, send out a memorandum telling your staff what's going on, and introduce the analyst personally to your key staff. If the analyst doesn't voluntarily take this up with you, be careful; you might be harboring an *agent provocateur*. (If, of course, you are against the whole project then you can capitalize on the analyst's lack of diplomacy and tact. Just send him into a hotbed of seething discontent and militant staff associations and unions without warning him.)

There are five golden rules for a successful investigation:

— BE OBJECTIVE
— VALIDATE
— GET *ALL* THE FACTS
— FOLLOW THROUGH
— BE DIPLOMATIC

79

If the analyst breaks any of these rules, then it is likely that the investigation will be incomplete, or the information gathered erroneous. You can co-operate with the analyst during the investigation by helping him to follow these rules.

Objectivity and validation: This means seeing things as they really are, not as either you or the analyst would like them to be.

Human nature being what it is, the analyst may collect and interpret only information which supports his theories. If he has done a similar job in another part of the organization or a different company, he might see this job as being like the previous one, without discovering the special factors which make it different. Similarly, you might day-dream about what you would like to happen—the analyst taking this as what *does* happen.

Validation is tied in with objectivity. The analyst must take reasonable steps to check all information. Perhaps he asks the same question in two different ways on two occasions. He sees if the pieces of the jig-saw puzzle fit into place or whether they have to be forced. (The worst case, of course, is getting the whole puzzle in place and having one piece left over.) The analyst doesn't go through this checking process because he thinks everybody in the organization is a liar.

We analyzed one of our projects to see how confusion had occurred:

— Three cases of blatant lying because users were against their management, or because they were scared of the project.

— The manager who told us:
the way he thought the system worked, or
the way he told the supervisor to do things, or
the way he wanted us to think it's done, or
the way he liked to think it should be done, or
the way it really happened.

— The worker who told us:
the way he was told to do things
the way he thought his boss would like him to tell us
the way he liked us to think it worked
the way that he actually did it
the way it said in the procedure manual, which was five
years out of date anyway.

— Two cases of unclarified terms. Manager X talked about
the 'ABC' document and Manager Y talked about the
'XYZ' document. Because of claimed 'confidentiality' no
samples were produced. It turned out that the documents
were the same; the name changed as they passed through
the organization. In the second case, sales said they
wanted sales figures broken down by territory; accounts
and production also wanted the report by territory. It
turned out that there were two different interpretations
of 'territory'.

— Distortion. Mr X talked for a half-hour on the importance
of having a missed delivery report, every day, 100 per
cent accurate. The report was later referred to by
Mr X as 'RUBBISH'. Reason: the morning we visited
him he had received a blast from his boss for missed
delivery to a very important client—the first and last
time it happened in ten years.

Each of the above cases required validation to determine the
real truth. Of course, the analyst can soldier on in the face of
adversity. But if you really want the project to succeed, you can
be a great help in fostering objectivity.

Follow through means that the analyst traces every item of data
to its ultimate destination, even though it lies outside the boundaries of the project. Otherwise the new system might starve other
parts of the organization of valuable data, because the new system
doesn't produce key documents as the old one did.

Be diplomatic: You'll know what this one means if you've met someone who wasn't. He is the guy who tells you your job after five minutes, argues, criticizes, and suggests things you discarded ten years ago. He can be the analyst who takes sides in internal politics, or the one who goes around making it clear he's God's gift to the organization. Or the man who says computers take the clerical drudgery out of work, to a group of clerks who spend their entire day doing clerical drudgery. If you get a man like this, get rid of him.

Those are the key aspects of the investigation part of the analyst's job, and how you can help—or hinder. The next chapter discusses what he does with all the information when he's got it.

10

Analyze, Hypothesize, Synthesize and Solutionize

The user request, feasibility study and detailed investigation have all been leading up to the design of the new system. The mass of information collected during the investigation has to be studied and sifted. A design brief must be prepared which contains:

— *objectives*: what the new system must achieve
— *boundaries and constraints*: what the new system must not do
— *time-scale*: when it has to be implemented and running
— *mandatory reports*: future information requirements specified by user managers; reports which the system *must* produce
— *essential processes*: what the new system *must* do
— *problems*: faults in the existing environment which must be cured in the new system
— *data/people/procedures*: what happens in the existing system and what is available for use in the new system

The design brief specifies *what* has to be done in the new system. System-design is figuring out *how* the new system will do it. If the problems in the existing system aren't specified, they will be carried over into the new system. As many have found to their cost, a computerized problem can be far worse than a manual one. So, if the new system is to be more than just the computerization of the existing system, requirements must be carefully analyzed before design. Some companies put great emphasis on the analysis step and have a formal checkpoint before design begins. This is equivalent to asking 'Do you agree that this is what the new system should and shouldn't do? Do you agree that these problems must be solved? Is our understanding of your environment correct?' Agreement on these points can be invaluable before starting design. All effort is then put into designing a solution to the right problem.

THE DESIGN APPROACH

The quality of the design will depend on many factors: the amount and quality of the preparatory work, the constraints on what the designer can and cannot do, and the experience and attitude of the designer.

A computer-based system is a mixture of computer processing and manual procedures. Many of the latter will take place in the user area and some in the computer area. For example, most computer systems operate in three steps. The first is the *input sub-system* which is concerned with handling data before it reaches the computer. All systems start with *data collection* or *data capture*: some event occurs, and details are recorded. The event could be someone clocking in for work in the morning, a customer placing an order, a payment being received, or a job being completed on the factory floor. The form in which the data is recorded will depend on the type of system. The majority of systems in operation today still rely on someone (clerk, manager, salesman, factory worker) filling in a form. Other systems use more sophisticated techniques, such as plastic badges or forms which can be read directly by machine, entering details via an on-line typewriter, or even automatic punching of a paper tape as receipts are rung up on a cash register. In systems which rely on the completion of forms the *source documents* will need to be checked manually for completeness, accuracy, and legibility. They will then be passed to the data preparation section where the details are transcribed onto the computer input media: punched cards or paper tape, or encoding onto magnetic tape. In addition to these procedures and forms, controls will be needed to guarantee the integrity of the data. Only after all this work has been done will the input pass to the next step, the *computer sub-system*.

The first step in the computer sub-system will be some form of edit program. This performs basic checks on the quality of the input data. Errors are listed out on a report; there will then be additional manual procedures to correct the errors and re-submit the input. Once okayed, the data then passes into the computer processing. Most computer processing is concerned with handling *files*. The computer creates these files, updates them, matches, and merges them; data will be extracted from the files and calculations will be done and eventually reports produced. The reports from the computer pass into the *output sub-system*.

Reports are usually produced on continuous stationery. A number of operations may be necessary to get the output into a usable form: decollating multi-part sets, bursting the continuous paper to form separate documents, trimming off the sprocket holes, folding, putting copies into binders or envelopes, sending it out. Quality control checks have to be done. Lastly, of course, procedures must be designed for *USE* of the output.

There is a mixture of machine and manual processes. *Getting the right balance between people and machine is one of the most important aspects of designing a computer system*; it is also the hardest.

A machine-biased system is one in which the design is formed in accordance with what the machine is doing and how. The way that people will work in the system depends on the way the machine is going to work. For example:

— input documents are complex and have to be prepared according to very strict rules, to suit the computer.

— great reliance is placed on long unwieldy codes, ideal for the computer to handle.

— there is a very rigid, tight timetable for sending the input to the computer, based on when the computer is scheduled to handle it.

It's this type of system which is greeted with 'it's too difficult to operate' or, 'it was simpler before, now we're expected to work like machines'. A machine-biased system has one and only one advantage: it will give very efficient computer processing.

A people-biased system has none of the characteristics listed above. There can be little or no change in methods, and the inputs and outputs will be geared to the aptitude and attitude of the people. It will be easy to use, but very expensive.

In some cases there has to be a bias toward either people or machine because of the very nature of the business and the way it operates. In one company, for example, the attitude and aptitude of the majority of the staff for paper work was very poor; they were craftsmen. This was a constraint when it came to designing the new system. We couldn't change the people, their attitude, or their aptitude. The new system had to be people-biased. Another company had good clerical people but very limited computer facilities and the designer was told: you can't change the machine. The new system had to be machine-biased to do the work on the small computer.

To illustrate this, we saw a computer system transferred lock, stock, and barrel from the head office of a large company to an overseas subsidiary. In the head office it worked well, but in the subsidiary it was nothing less than a disaster. For example, the date was very important and had to appear on most input documents. The head office used the month-day-year method:

$$0\ 7\ 0\ 3\ 7\ 0$$

for 3 July 1970. This form of date is best for the computer to handle. In the exported system every conceivable form of date was presented for input:

7 / 3 / 7 0
0 3 0 7 7 0
3 J U L 7 0
J U L 3 7 0

All these formats were rejected by the computer, with the exception of the second, which was taken as 7 March 1970. No amount of persuasion could get the staff to follow the rules. So the computer system was modified to accept free-form input. This required a bigger and more complex program. With similar alterations being made all through the system, the computer had to be up-graded to a bigger model.

A related design problem is to decide where computer processing should stop and manual processing take over. Here are three extreme examples to illustrate this point:

1. In one company an old Chairman of the Board, long since retired, had been a volunteer fireman. He had established a fund for widows and dependents of volunteer firemen killed in the line of duty before 1928. (Nobody remembers why 1928 was the cut-off date.) Employees of the company could elect to have contributions deducted automatically from their pay checks. When the payroll went on the computer, this feature went with it, costing about $500 to do all the work. Last year, deductions amounted to $3.37. Assuming the whole thing couldn't have been forgotten, a non-computer alternative (send the office-boy around with a collecting cup once a year?) would have been infinitely more sensible.

2. Some years ago, the Post Office Savings Accounts in the United Kingdom were computerized. There were some 40 million accounts, about half of which were 'active'. Under special legal provisions it was possible for a patriotic saver to donate the interest on his account to the Chancellor of the Exchequer to help pay off the National Debt. Less than 200 loyal investors took this option. The original design for the computer system incorporated facilities to cater for it. It was, we understand, an Organization

and Methods man who pointed out a workable alternative.

3. A company was putting in an open-item invoicing system. This required payments made to the company to be matched with actual invoice amounts on the sales ledger. Customers were asked to quote the invoice numbers which matched their payment check. Most were very co-operative and did so. The analyst (rightly) considered those cases where only a check was sent, but no corresponding invoice identification. A very complex program was written which took an unidentified payment and matched it against all invoice values for that customer. If no match was found then a second search was made to see if the payment was for two invoice amounts, and so on. Everyone agreed after the event that a better idea would have been to have a girl go through all unidentified payments manually, something which would have taken a tenth of the cost and a quarter of the time.

The secret of good design is not to become captivated by the technology of the design—what the computer *can* do—to the detriment of plain, straightforward common-sense. One argument which will be used by the technicians is that 'hardware costs are coming down, so we can now do things on the machine which weren't financially viable in the past'. Beware of this one; it's great in theory but can be nonsense in practice.

Another common design fault is trying to get the people to fit the system, forgetting that people can't always be changed. Codes are a good example. Computers operate better with codes than with narrative descriptions. Many consumers (over which the company has no control) prefer to deal with descriptions rather than codes. (Imposing codes has been one of the reasons why computers have had a bad public press.) For example, one insurance company completely computerized its records and asked all clients to quote their code on all correspondence—all 124 characters of it. In another case, a publishing company put its orders on the computer and asked all customers to quote the International Standard Book Number and/or Library of Congress

Catalog Card Number. When this (naturally) didn't quite work, the company went back to taking orders by title/author but didn't change the computer system; they created a team of six clerks who coded the orders before they went to the computer.

Other factors which influence the design are:

— *The background of the designer*: If the man designing the system is an ex-programmer of long standing without much experience of systems work, his personal bias is bound to be towards the computer. You don't spend four to five years programming without thinking of the computer rather than people.

— *Lack of knowledge about the user area*: This is a direct result of poor preparatory work. If the designer doesn't know the attitude and aptitude of the people, and the jobs they do, how can he design for the environment?

— *Lack of user involvement*: The user can bring the designer away from the machine to think about his people and their environment. But this requires getting involved by studying the specifications for the new system, not blind acceptance of all the ideas put up by the designer.

— *Design sequence*: The designer works on the outputs, then designs the computer processing and files to give the output, and finally develops the input to feed the computer sub-system. This results in the rationalization of the inputs around the machine. Design is a cyclical process, refining designs and making sure that the inputs, outputs and files are compatible.

Reaching an equitable balance between man and machine can be largely a matter of compromise, and this means consultations and involvement on both sides.

THE SYSTEM SPECIFICATION

This is the formal output from systems design. It is the master description of the new system: the inputs and input procedures, the computer processing and the files, the outputs and all their associated procedures. The specification must be studied and approved by everyone who will be involved in further development work and running the system:

— *users*: Does it do what you wanted? Are the inputs and outputs OK? Are the procedures suitable for your people?
— *programming*: Is the machine processing possible? Are the requirements for computer processing clearly and unambiguously stated?
— *computer operations and data preparation*: Is the system capable of operation? Are all the facilities available when required? Are the requirements clearly stated?

And so on. The systems specification checkpoint is a very important one. It is the last major review before the high cost tasks of programming, testing, conversion and implementation. Changes to the specification after work begins on these tasks can be very expensive indeed. It's like building a house. If you change the specification before a brick is laid or a hole is dug, lines are redrawn on a plan. If you decide the kitchen should be where the bathroom is when the house is half built, they have to tear it down and start over again.

With a checkpoint as important as this, the user must be able to understand the system specification. It mustn't be full of technical mumbo-jumbo. You must have the time to study and understand it.

This is also the last chance for changing the detailed cost/ benefit analysis. Now that the work has progressed, the estimates given in the feasibility study can be made definite. It is a brave man who raises his hand at this point and says 'Stop!' But now is the time to get the system right, or perhaps to say 'No' altogether; at least you will be cutting your losses. You won't be popular if you do, but if the cost estimates have gone spiralling upwards and the claimed benefits have dwindled downwards, don't soldier on with a lost cause.

LOOKING AHEAD

The system specification describes the new system. Remember, however, that major tasks are still to come: writing and testing the programs, testing the system as a whole, preparing the people and the files for the new system, and actually effecting the changeover. Never accept a system without seeing plans, schedules and costs for this work. Now the new system is defined in detail, these plans can be formulated in full. Your people will be actively concerned later, and you should have as much advance warning as possible as to who, how, what, where, and when.

11

How Not to Lose Your Job

The basic assumption of this chapter is that you *don't* want to lose your job when the new computer system comes in. If you want nothing to do with it and prefer to quit, or wait until you're let go, and seek a job elsewhere—fine. This chapter is for those who want to keep on working for their company, but who are a bit doubtful about the future.

First of all, some reassurance. Based on statistical averages, if you are a clerical or shop-floor worker, it is unlikely that you will be eliminated by the computer; it could happen, but the odds are against it. If you are a supervisor or in management, it is *extremely* unlikely. This is a matter of history.

Now, there are two possible dangers to your job. The first is technological and the second is political. We'll discuss them in that order.

THE TECHNOLOGICAL THREAT

You've got to be doing a repetitive clerical job before the computer will interfere with your job security, such as typing invoices in a typing-pool, or up-dating a ledger on manual cards. The computer may do these tasks. But remember there will still be jobs getting the input cleaned up before sending it to the computer, dealing with queries, handling the output. Some people may be transferred or fired; those left will have more responsibility and even more job security when the computer system goes in.

Perhaps the computer is planned to make better use of the resources; more work with less plant and people. If the computer is going to optimize delivery routes so that all deliveries can be done with 25 per cent fewer vehicles, what's going to happen to the 25 per cent of drivers and vehicles? Get rid of them, right? Wrong. Given this type of delivery service, the business is going to increase. It's really a question of *no extra* staff or vehicles.

Perhaps they don't need you, or anyone with your skills, anymore. The only alternative is to develop new skills. It may take several years to get the new system in the air, and some time after that before they are sure it is working properly in all its parts. That is the time you need a) to change your skills and b) to make yourself indispensable.

Your starting advantage is that you know how things are done the old way. If you are asked for information and help about it, be as co-operative as possible. If there is a position available as 'liaison with data processing' or the equivalent, try to get it. If there is a committee being set up, try to get on it. Work as closely with the data processing people as possible, and make sure management knows it. There are two reasons for this. The first is that it is difficult to fire someone who has been helpful. When it comes to discussing the employees and deciding who will have to go, it is easier to fire someone who has been against the computer system and has been making trouble than it is to fire someone who is in favor of it. (If you took any of the advice in Chapter 5 on 'How Not to Have a Computer', don't worry. Once you accept that the computer is inevitable and start being co-operative, past sins will be forgotten. You can even turn this to advantage by letting yourself be converted. Your opposition was rational, but having considered all the alternatives, your support is rational too. You are a clear thinker, not swayed by the fads of the moment. Etc etc.) The second advantage in working with the computer people is that you are in the best possible position to learn new skills.

Perhaps your job is going to be eliminated, so you have to learn something new. If you opt for a job in another department, maybe that one will be next on the list for a computer system. No; you must aim to get yourself transferred to the computer department or some unit connected with it. Here is real job security. Plus, like as not, more pay and prestige.

The only rule for learning about computers generally and a particular job skill, such as systems analysis, is that *you must not be seen to be doing it on your own*. Buy books and read them, yes. But don't take the books to the office (not until you've got the new job sewn up). Do not under any circumstances pay your own money for a course on computers. This is a last resort, a desperation measure, and will be recognized as such. *Get the company to give you the training*. Not only will the training be better but, once they have invested the time and money in you, they will be reluctant to let you go without getting something back—i.e. work from you in the data processing department, or in your old department, helping to run the computer system. So if there are any courses, seminars, films, or what-have-you going on, do everything possible to get on them.

And in the meantime, soak up everything you can from the computer people. They have more influence than you think (and more than they should) in making recommendations for the new jobs that will be created for the computer system. If you have proven yourself bright and adaptable, your name will be first on their lips when management asks who will be best for the new job of data-controller, or key punch supervisor, or file librarian, or data clerk, or shift supervisor, or whatever jobs are going.

If you still can't bring yourself to favor the computer, and learn new skills, there is another path open, but it is more risky. (The exception would be if you have tenure, absolute job security, by contract or union rules or company policy; in that case, all you have to do is sit tight.) Otherwise, you might try to set yourself up as *the* anti-computer person. You might be able to convince your bosses that having one dissenter around is a good thing, it keeps everything in perspective. Along with this, all duties having to do with the computer will have to be delegated by you to people below you, which is one way of increasing your staff, and therefore your power, and thus hold on to your job. More often than not, however, this attempt backfires. So if you're determined to try it, be prepared to change your employer for a new one.

THE POLITICAL THREAT

Supervisors and managers are less likely to become technologically obsolescent; their job skills are not among those a computer can do well. The major threat to you, if you are in this group, is a political one.

For example, departmental and/or company reorganizations may accompany a new computer system. Jobs are being eliminated or combined. Maybe yours will be one of those done away with. Or possibly you have a rival, both of you gunning for the boss's job when he moves up. The computer system becomes another factor in the political struggling.

However the computer manifests itself as a political tool, one thing is clear: *this is a political situation like any other political situation.* If you don't want to play politics, the best rule is to lie low and keep your mouth shut. Don't give an opinion. Move with the majority, and don't make any outstanding mistakes. Even then, if the politicians are really vicious ones, you may become a victim.

If you do want to play politics, then good luck to you, but we can't advise that. Some men have got to the top of the company by the political route, and with no other skills whatsoever; but they are the exceptions. In the political jungle you are on your own, and the computer really has very little to do with it.

Osborn

12

The Care and Feeding of Programmers

Programming is a job that did not exist thirty years ago. Today, every company that owns a computer has at least one programmer; big companies may have hundreds. Because people in other departments usually do not come into contact with them, who programmers are and what their job requires is sometimes mysterious. In this chapter, we shall try to remove some of that mystery. (As with other people connected with computers, the programmers themselves may not like it because they prefer to walk the corridors clothed in mystery; it makes them feel important.)

Programmers are the people who write instructions for the computer. A computer can't think; it mechanically performs a sequence of instructions exactly as they are written. If there is a mistake, it will blindly follow the wrong instruction. An average program can contain thousands of instructions, all of which must be precisely correct, down to the last dot and comma, for the program to work correctly. It's impossible for any human to write programs which do not, at first, contain mistakes. That's what makes programming such a difficult job and, for some people, a fascinating one; the challenge of making the fewest possible mistakes the first time round, and then, by putting the program through a series of dry runs, tests, finding the ones that are left. If the programmer is good and is allowed enough time to test his programs thoroughly, the finished product will be perfect. If it's allowed to operate on real data before all the bugs are fixed, disaster can strike. It's a program bug, *not* a computer error, that makes your electricity bill $999999.99 or sends you ten subscriptions to a magazine instead of one, or fails to credit a payment you've made. It was a program bug that wrecked an unmanned rocket a few years ago; a programmer had left out just one comma, and failed to find the mistake during testing.

Before we look at the job of the programmer and how his work fits in with the system development project, we must first have a closer look at the nature of a computer program.

A program is a series of coded instructions. These instructions are loaded into the memory of the computer from cards, paper tape, magnetic tape, or magnetic disk. When the instructions are loaded, the operator initiates the program and the first instruction is analyzed by the computer hardware and appropriate action taken. This action could be to read a data card, read a record from magnetic disk, move data around the computer memory, add two numbers together. The operations which the computer can perform are these very simple actions. When the action specified in one program instruction has been taken, the next instruction automatically follows, then the next, followed by the next, and so on until the last instruction is reached. This one will be some form of a 'halt' instruction which notifies the operator that the job is finished (EOJ—End Of Job) or that an error has occurred. The operator then takes appropriate action, such as unloading the input, output, and files, deleting the program, and going on to the next job.

The two important things to notice about the operation of a program are the simplicity of the operations performed by the computer, and the automatic sequence in which the instructions are analyzed and obeyed. The operator starts the job and the computer executes it without further operator intervention. All that the operator will do during the job is to load more paper onto the line-printer as required, keep the card-reader supplied with punched cards to be read, and load or unload magnetic tapes and disks as needed.

Normally, the computer obeys the instructions in the sequence in which they are written. Take a very simple series of computer instructions (in which the numbers are memory addresses):

ADD 09 TO 10
ADD 10 TO 11
ADD 11 TO 12
DIVIDE 12 BY 13

These programmed instructions are shown in a simple narrative form; inside the computer they would consist of series of numeric-based special codes that the computer can understand. The numbers 09, 10, 11, 12, and 13 relate to memory addresses, that is storage compartments in the memory of the computer. If the contents of the storage locations were 8, 5, 9, 8, and 3 respectively, this simple extract from a program would calculate the average of three values. The sequence of operations performed by the computer would be:

Start
address:	09	10	11	12	13
contents:	8	5	9	8	3

ADD 09 TO 10
address:	09	10	11	12	13
contents:	8	13	9	8	3

Note that the contents of 10 (5) are replaced with the result of the computer's operation (13).

ADD 10 TO 11
address:	09	10	11	12	13
contents:	8	13	22	8	3

Again the contents of 10 (13) are added to the contents of 11 (9) and the result (22) is put into 11.

ADD 11 TO 12

address:	09	10	11	12	13
contents:	8	13	22	30	3

The result is to add the contents of 11 (22) to the contents of 12 (8) and put the sum (30) in 12.

DIVIDE 12 BY 13

address:	09	10	11	12	13
contents:	8	13	22	30	10

The contents of 12 (30) are divided by the contents of 13 (3) and the result (10) placed in 13.

This is, of course, only part of the program. Further instructions will be necessary to read in the data values to be processed—i.e. reading a card or cards which contain the values 8, 5, 9, 8, 3, etc—and further instructions to get the result out—that is, to print it. Each instruction is held in the computer as a series of special number codes. The programmer, however, writes the instructions using a programming language, as discussed later.

Programming would be a very simple matter indeed if all the programmer had to do was write a series of instructions which would be obeyed one after another. The complexity of programming arises through the use of a special type of instruction called a *branch* or *jump* instruction. This is a means of varying the sequence in which instructions are obeyed. The branch instructions enable simple conditions or states within the computer to be tested, and different courses of action may be taken, depending on the value of the condition or state.

One way of showing this conditional logic is by means of a flowchart. This is a diagrammatic representation of the logic of a program. There are many different symbols which can be used, but there are only two which are really necessary:

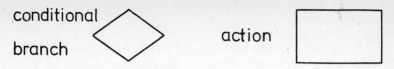

conditional branch

action

The diamond represents a test of a particular condition. The condition tested is written inside it and the values of the condition are shown outside. Lines are used to link the exits of the diamonds to the action boxes.

Here's an example. A stock transaction record is read into the computer from punched cards. Each stock transaction record might be an issue of a quantity in stock, in which case it has an 'I' code punched, or a receipt of a quantity into stock, which

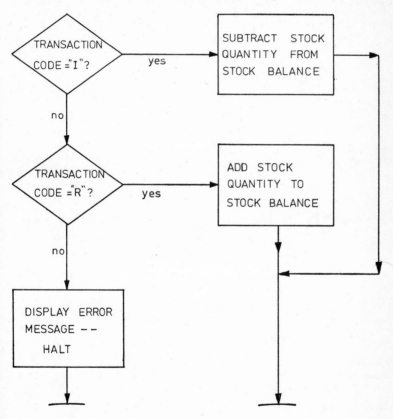

will have an 'R' punched. If an 'I' is punched, the quantity issued is to be *subtracted* from the stock balance of the product (which is held on magnetic disk). If an 'R' is punched, the quantity received is to be added to the stock balance on disk for the product. This would be shown thus on the flowchart on page 96.

The two statements in the diamonds would be branch instructions in the program. In simple narrative form, the program could be written thus:

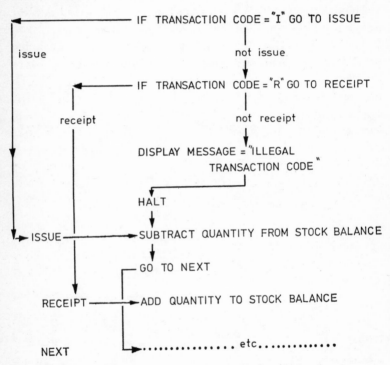

Again, these instructions are in a narrative form for human understanding. In the computer there would be a series of numeric-coded instructions.

So now on to the job of the programmer.

The starting-point is the program specification. This states *what* the program is to do; the programmer figures out *how*. The programmer needs to know not only what the program must do, but also the data to be used:

— the format and content of the input
— the format and content of the output
— the format and content of the files.

When the overall system is designed, one program specification must be prepared for each program in the system. *Once programming is begun, changes to the specification are very expensive.*

The programmer studies the specification, checking its completeness and clarity. He then plans the logic of the program, probably by drawing a series of flowcharts. This means that he must break the total job down into a series of simple computer-oriented actions with the appropriate conditional branches. This in itself can be difficult. For example, imagine your car is in the garage. List the sequence of actions to drive to work. Start by assuming you're in the garage:

1. Open car door
2. Sit down
3. Put ignition key in ignition
4. Turn on ignition
5. Engage first gear
6. Release handrake
7. Clutch etc

Give this list to somebody and ask them to follow the instructions exactly (as would a computer) and you'll be in trouble:

— what happens if he doesn't have the car door key?
— how about getting in the car before sitting down?
— what happens if there is no ignition key?
— what about the car facing a wall and smashing into it?
— or opening the garage door?

And so on. Breaking a major complex task down into a step-by-step procedure with conditional tests is not an easy task. The rule for constructing a computer program is to break the overall task down into the *lowest* series of actions. Remember the computer will act exactly as instructed.

The logic of the flowchart is desk-checked by 'dry-running'—that is, following through the paths with simple test data. When the programmer is satisfied with the logic, he begins the next step, coding.

All commercial programs are written in a programming language which is biased toward the human. This means that the programmer writes a program as a series of simple statements called a *source program*. One language that can be used is COBOL —COmmon Business Oriented Language, another is FORTRAN —FORmular TRANslation. COBOL can be used for general business programs; the program statements are written in English-type sentences, grouped to form paragraphs. Here are a few COBOL statements, out of context:

    READ NUMBER
    SUBTRACT ISSUE FROM STOCK-ON-HAND
       GIVING BALANCE
    WRITE LINE 1 BEFORE ADVANCING ONE PAGE
    IF STOCK NOT EQUAL TO MINIMUM GO TO
       STOCK PROCESS

An example of how these statements can be organized into a program will be given later in the chapter.

FORTRAN is used for mathematical or scientific applications. Example statements, chosen at random, are:

$$I = 3$$
$$READ\ 4,R$$
$$C = 2 * 3.1416 * R$$
$$PRINT\ 2,\ R,\ C$$
$$IF(I-5)6$$

Each of these statements will generate an instruction (or series of instructions) in the appropriate number-coded computer form.

The coded source program is prepared for input, punched into cards or paper tape. The next step is compilation. The source program is input to the computer with a special translator program, *the compiler*. This converts the programmer-oriented source program into the machine-oriented *object program*. The object program is the series of machine-code instructions which will be input to the computer and executed with the live data to produce results. The compilation process produces listings of the program.

The program has to be written according to very strict rules and regulations of word choice, grammar, punctuation, and syntax. If the programmer breaks any of the rules, the compiler in the machine will not be able to understand the programmer's intentions. The errors will be noted on the listing as diagnostics— error messages. Let's take a simple example of a poorly coded program:

1		IF TRANSACTION CODE='I' GO TO ISSUE.
2		IF TRANSACTION CODE='R GO TO RECEIVED.
3		DISPLAY MESSAGE='ILLEGAL.
4		TRANSACTION CODE'.
5		HALT
6	ISSUE	SUBTRACT QUANTITY FROM STOCK BALANCE.
7		GO TO NEXT.
8	RECEIPT	ADO QUANTITY TO STOCK BALANCE.
9	NEXT	....

The errors in this programming language are as follows:

Statement number	Rule/Format
1	Illegal verb: IF instead of IF
2	No closing quotation mark: 'R instead of 'R'

3	Each statement must end with a full stop. In this case the message is read as 'ILLEGAL.; no closing quotation
4	Carrying on from (3) TRANSACTION CODE' is a meaningless statement with no verb
5	No full stop after HALT
8	Illegal verb. There is no such verb as ADO, should be ADD

There is another error in statement 2, although we can't be certain of this without seeing the whole of the program coding. The words 'ISSUE' and 'RECEIPT' are called labels or tags. If in the complete program there is no label 'RECEIVED', statement (2) is thus an error which will show up as a diagnostic thus:

2   IF TRANSACTION CODE='R' GO TO
       RECEIVED
       ****
       **UNMATCHED LABEL

Thus, in this example, if the code is R, the compiler won't know where to go, because there is no label 'RECEIVED'.

So the programmer's first task is to get a clean listing; all the clerical coding errors have to be located and corrected.

The next step is program testing, proving that the program works according to the specification and that the *logic* is correct. The compiler will note infringements of the language rules. It won't be able to detect errors in logic. Take the example program again:

1	IF TRANSACTION CODE='R' GO TO ISSUE.
2	IF TRANSACTION CODE='I' GO TO RECEIPT.
3	DISPLAY MESSAGE='ILLEGAL
4	TRANSACTION CODE'.
5	HALT.

6 ISSUE   SUBTRACT QUANTITY FROM STOCK BALANCE.

7   GO TO ISSUE.

8 RECEIPT   ADD QUANTITY TO STOCK BALANCE.

9 NEXT   ....

This program will pass every test that the compiler will make. But the logic is, to put it mildly, rubbish! The mistakes are as follows:

1. The labels in statements (1) and (2) are mixed-up. If a receipt comes in coded 'R' the program will go to ISSUE. This means that the received quantity of goods will be subtracted from the stock balance.

2. The code is written as '1' (one) as opposed to 'I'. If an issue comes in marked 'I' it will fail the test in (2)— IS CODE=1 . . . and an error message will be displayed when the input is OK.

3. Let's assume that we get referred to step (6). The subtraction takes place. The next instruction is then done: GO TO ISSUE. The program would then go into an endless loop: back to (6), to (7), to (6), to (7), and so on until the value of stock balance would get so low that the computer couldn't store the required number of decimal points. The program might pass the compiler checks but it is useless for processing. The computer can't possibly know that, of course, 1 should be I. 'It is ridiculous to add issues—they should be subtracted.' It is up to the programmer to get the logic right. He must follow the logic through (dry running again), and then run the program with carefully made-up test data. The results are compared with the requirements of the specification.

After each of the programs is tested against the original specification, the group of programs for a complete job is tested together, checking that the output of one program is acceptable as input to another, and so on. When this is done, the programs are ready for full systems testing, as described in the next chapter.

We have used simple examples to illustrate the job of programming. Real programs are much more complicated; one may have a thousand instructions, processing four different types of input, handling three files, producing two or three reports. Such a program may have two or three hundred branch instructions.

Some people think that after a couple of years, programming is a boring clerical job. One user, after finding out about the job of a programmer, said 'No wonder they're a bit funny—you know, twisted in the way they think. Breaking everything down into those simple logical precise steps.'

SOFTWARE

The computer industry, like many others, has invented new terms that, over the years, have taken on different meanings. Software is an example of this. Originally, software meant any program written for the computer. In common usage today it has also taken on a narrower meaning: a program which has been written or tested by some outside agency or organization. The term 'software package' is sometimes used in this context. A company can acquire a program from some outside source and thus save themselves the time and trouble of writing it themselves. Examples of 'packaged' software are:

- operating systems
- programming languages
- general utilities
- sub-routines
- generalized file processors
- application packages

These are described below.

Many installations have similar types of jobs to do on the computer. For example, many use the programming language COBOL. Each installation will need a compiler program to convert the English-like source program to the machine-coded program. The writing of such a compiler is a very time-consuming and specialized task. Instead of each installation producing its own compiler, the computer manufacturer will provide a compiler for general use by all installations.

Most software is produced by computer manufacturers, although some is supplied by specialist 'software houses' and trade associations. Some very large companies have a 'software group' which produces software for internal use by decentralized computer departments. The programs in the software package are supplied punched in cards or paper tape, or recorded on magnetic disks or magnetic tape, ready for use.

Operating system: Also called the Executive. A master control program which looks after input/output operations, finds programs in an on-line library, loads and starts them, facilitates operator/machine communication via the console typewriter, produces accounting information on computer time usage, and controls multiprogramming (running more than one program in the computer).

General utilities: Complete pre-written programs which do common jobs such as sorting records and transcribing data from one form to another, eg punched cards to magnetic disk, magnetic tape to printer.

Sub-routines: Small units of coding which can be used in a program to do common tasks: finding a cube root, producing a standard pattern on a graph-plotter or line-printer.

Generalized file processors/Data Base Management Systems: These are a combination of programming languages and general utilities. GFPs and DBMSs are groups of programs which can be used for setting up, processing, and getting data from computer-based files.

Application packages: The payroll system in one company is very much like a payroll system in other companies. Why should each write its own programs? An application package is one solution; a group of pre-written and tested programs which do the computer processing for a particular commercial or industrial job. Other examples are stock control, production control, order processing, invoicing, and sales accounting.

No company thinking of using a computer evaluates only the hardware; as much attention is given to the range of software available as to the efficiency, reliability, and cost of the hardware.

prove it
to me!

MISSOURI

13

Prove It to Me

Program testing should have proved the logic of the programs against the specifications. The next step is to test the system as a whole. It must be shown that the output of one program is acceptable to the next, and that all associated manual procedures work both in the user area and in data processing. Program testing went on in isolation; systems testing should take place in a real-life environment, with you, the user, participating. Now is the time when any inadequacies in the earlier stages of the work will come to light.

The approach to systems testing is very important. To start testing with the wrong objectives can be costly. The systems specification is the final checkpoint before programming, testing, and implementation. The first objective of systems testing is to *prove the system against the systems specification* and incidentally to see if data conditions arise which aren't catered for in the specification. The primary objective *should not* be to see if the specification is right. This can be shutting the barn door after the horse has bolted, because the specification *should* have been right before programming ever began. Certainly, testing may reveal inadequacies in the systems specification. But, if you are reviewing a specification, imagine that there will be no testing; if the system were to go in as described, would it work? Testing is an opportunity to prove the system, not design it.

PLANNING

Planning for systems testing should have begun long ago. The feasibility report should have a brief outline plan for it. The plans should be finalized while programming is going on. You will be asked to supply sample cases to use as test data, and to help check out the results of the tests. You should be given plenty of advance warning; what will be required when, and how much time you will have to devote to it. If it is a large project, you might have to get in extra people (they may be needed during implementation, too—see the next chapter) in order to be able to keep on with your day-to-day work at the same time.

The detailed test plan should include:

— general outline of the approach
— schedule of tests
— for each test: data to be used, conditions being tested, and samples of the expected output

'Data to be used' and 'expected output' do *not* mean just a vague description, but actual samples. If these have not been prepared, you should insist that systems testing be put off until they are. Without them the testing will be haphazard, and when the systems analyst declares that the system is 'tested' and ready to begin operational running, you have no proof that it is. The first few cycles of real running are very likely to be chaotic and be of no use to you.

The testing should be as concerned with errors and exceptions as with ordinary cases, if not more so. As a guideline, we offer the following checklist of the kinds of things that should be tested:

— records with all the data set to zero
— incorrect input of all types
— correcting and re-submitting input
— invalid combinations of input
— input that does not match the files

— all re-start and by-pass routines
— recreating files after they are destroyed
— all combinations of end-of-file conditions
— handling output errors
— all error messages

Your attitude throughout systems testing, and especially in gathering together sample data for the systems analyst to use in testing, should be—*prove it to me*. Tell them you are from Missouri, you're a doubting Thomas, a disbeliever, a nullifidian. You don't believe the system will work, and the test cases you choose are designed to catch it out. But don't include totally unrealistic test cases. If a test case isn't catered for in the specification, why didn't you query it earlier?

Only a few medical and military systems can cater for 100 per cent of the eventualities. We met a systems analyst in a bar who was close to homicide after one and a half years of systems testing. On hearing his sad tale, we sympathized with him. One or two users had taken a smug pleasure in putting in totally unrealistic data which easily beat the system. He had spent the last year adding unnecessary routines; by the time the system went on the air, the programs would be five times as big as they would need to be. Both the users and the analyst were taking the wrong approach. They should have been testing for what was right and rejecting everything else.

Keep the same attitude in checking the results. After each test, compare the actual output with the sample expected output drawn up beforehand. You are looking for discrepancies, and pounce on each one with a glad little cry. It is up to the systems people to find out what caused the discrepancy, fix it, and run the test again. Do not let them get away with assurances that it is fixed—you should see the new test and see for yourself that the actual output is now identical with that expected. (You should have your own copies of the expected output; it has not been unknown for a systems analyst to change *that* rather than the bug.)

It could be your fault, if you were given the systems specification

119

to review and just skimmed over it because it looked complicated or because you were being pressured to initial the thing so they could get on with it. Or it could be their fault for not giving you the whole story at that time.

If it appears during systems testing that the specification is substantially incorrect, the best course is to abandon the testing for the time being and clear up what the system *should* be doing first. Then, when the programs are fixed, you can go back to testing to see if it is doing that. This is obviously going to be time-consuming and very expensive. The best course of all is not to let it happen in the first place.

Systems testing must use limited quantities of data. The files have to be small. If they were the size of operational files, the computer time needed for testing would be exorbitant. No matter how realistic you try to make it, it can't be exactly as it will be when it's the real thing. So systems testing, whether or not it's called that, can overlap into the first few cycles of operational running. This is discussed in the next chapter.

14

The Great Day

The great day is the day when the system 'goes live'. But it's not just a day with a red ring around it on the calendar, and it might not even be a single day at all, but a period of weeks or months. Going from a tested system to an operational system is not just a matter of pushing the right buttons; there's a lot of work to be done. The major tasks are:

— converting files
— training all staff who will be involved with the new system
— writing instruction manuals
— getting new forms printed
— installing any new hardware
— recruiting new staff, if necessary

The two biggest jobs are file conversion and user training. Before discussing those in more detail, however, it is necessary to describe the four possible methods of implementing a new system.

The parallel method

The principle of parallel running is that the new system is operated side-by-side with the old one for several cycles. If it is primarily a monthly system, this means for two to four months. The two sets of output are compared, and any discrepancies are tracked down. When the new system is proved to be operating correctly, the old one is discontinued. This also provides an opportunity for on-the-job training for everybody, before they get into the deep end.

For example, suppose sales analysis is going to be put on the computer. Under the old system, the manager and his secretary prepared the sales analysis reports with the help of an adding machine. For parallel running, they just keep on doing it, while the computer does it, too. The two sets of reports produced should be alike; they can be compared, and discrepancies tracked down, until all problems are solved.

In concept this is simple. In practice a number of difficulties may arise. First of all, it is unlikely that the two systems will be entirely identical, especially if the objectives of computerizing were to improve operation, provide better reports, and so on. So, if the outputs are identical, that's the time to get worried. In order to 'prove' the new system against the old one, some special temporary procedures may have to be put in. If the new system is very different, or if there is no counterpart at all because it wasn't being done before, then one of the other methods of implementation will have to be used.

Another difficulty may be that there is just too much work involved in running two systems at once. For example, if it's a production control system, you can't make everything twice; if it's invoicing, you may not have enough staff to keep on preparing the invoices the old way and provide input for the computer, too. Again, one of the other methods, or a compromise combination, may have to be used.

One important point to remember is that parallel running is *not* a substitute for systems testing. And it most certainly is not a substitute for having good system specifications in the first place. If the systems people try to make it so, the 'parallel run' can go on indefinitely. We know one company where so-called parallel running has been going on for eighteen months, with no end in sight. Any potential savings from the new system for the next five years have been eaten up by the extra costs.

The pilot method

A pilot conversion involves putting the system in, in its entirety, but only in one part of the company. This assumes that there are a number of places in the company where the system will eventually operate and that their procedures are similar. For example, if the company has a number of branches, one would be selected for the pilot; if there are several factories in different parts of the company doing things the same way, one would be used for the pilot operation. The advantage of this, of course, is that the computer people can concentrate their resources on the one place; after the out-of-town try-out, the other units get a tested, sure-fire system.

One project we worked on was a control system for a decentralized manufacturing company. There were six factories, at different places around the country. A pilot conversion was the logical approach. But the company's policy, for good or ill, was that each factory manager had complete autonomy. No one could tell one manager he had been chosen for the pilot, nor tell the others they weren't. Each of the six managers wanted his factory to have the system first; it was a matter of prestige. They had to fight it out among themselves; and a fight was what it was. They were locked in an office, like the College of Cardinals electing a Pope, and couldn't come out until they'd agreed. It took two days, one bloody nose, and three black eyes.

If you have the opportunity to be involved in a pilot run, try to be either the first or the third (or later) to get the system. The first one gets all the help; the third one gets a guaranteed, error-free system. Poor number two might get a system with some problems still remaining, but no help.

The gradual method

This means that the system becomes operational in phases. For example, suppose a retail organization were putting in a

sales-recording and ordering system. The sales-recording part—
new input for the computer system and sales analysis reports—
could be implemented first, with ordering still done the old way.
When this part of the system was proved to be working smoothly,
ordering could be started. Obviously, not all systems can be
designed to be implemented this way.

The immediate method

The old system stops on one evening and the new system begins
the next morning. Or else there is no equivalent manual system.
Otherwise known as the guts method. For example, an insurance
company introduced a new type of pension fund and a system
was developed. The new product was released on 1 January and
the new system went live at the same time. It was impractical to
set up a temporary manual system. In another case, a factory
went over to a radically new production control system, including
the allocation of jobs to available machines. The new system
provided daily schedules (as opposed to the old system which
was weekly) and the basic format of the source documents was
changed. The whole plant closed down for three weeks' vacation
in the summer. When the workers left, the old system was
abandoned; when they returned from holiday the new system
was used. The disadvantages of immediate conversion are obvious,
but there may be no feasible alternative. The major requirements
for the guts method are good testing, good training—and prayer.

To end this chapter, here are some important points about file
conversion and training.

FILE CONVERSION

Before the new system can be used, the computer-based files held
on magnetic disk or magnetic tape must be created. If you are
going from an old manual system to a new computer system this

will require more time and effort than going from, say, a punched card tabulator system to the computer. If the system involves the conversion of a large number of manual records to computer form, such as 50,000 customer account records or 100,000 part or product records, then file conversion may be the most expensive single step in the development project. There is more to it than just taking the manual records and passing them to data preparation for punching. The manual records may not be suitable as punching documents. The information to go on the computer file may be located in many different parts of the company. The data in the existing system may be incomplete or inaccurate. When the computer system is started, it is vital to have information as complete and accurate as possible. For example:

— In one manufacturing company, all units of a certain type were with stainless steel fittings, unless they were for export, in which case they had chrome fittings. Everybody in the factory knew this; it was never actually written down, but everybody could tell by looking at the customer's address. Everybody knew that is, except for the systems analyst. File conversion was rushed and the works order no longer showed the customer's name or his address. The scrap rate was enormous.

— In another company, a master set of parts description cards was maintained. Over the years many of the descriptions had changed but the people operating the manual system knew what was going on and never bothered to alter the cards. So there could be a card which said 'PART NUMBER 12345—$\frac{1}{2}''$ widget' but for the last two years it had been a $\frac{1}{4}''$ widget. The cards were taken and punched for the computer and thence written to disk to form the new computerized parts file. The part numbers were changed, however, to accommodate the computer. It took them six months to work their way out of the mess.

In the latter case there were howls from the user: 'We never

127

had all this rubbish in the old system. Blasted computers, always knew they were no damn good.' The 'rubbish' did exist in the old system, but it was flexible and people made allowances for the bad data. The computer was inflexible and no such allowances were made. So the process of file conversion needs to be carefully planned:

— What is the data required on the new file?
— What is the source in the existing system?
— If there are several sources, which is the most accurate? What cross-checks must be made?
— What is the document in the existing system? Can it be punched as it is or must it be transcribed onto special punching documents?
— What special programs, if any, must be written to create the new file?
— What checks are to be made on the input data? Who is to clarify and correct errors?

The majority of the work must be carried out by the user staff. They have more clerical resources than data processing, know the data better than anyone else, and it is their system.

The second major problem is work in progress. The activities of the company must go on. If you are converting a stock file which contains a stock balance (i.e. stock in hand in the ware-house) and stock movements are taking place every day, then the balance will be out of date at the very moment that you create a file record. One way of handling this problem would be to set up the record containing all the indicative information which is not subject to frequent change: the stock item number, the pack size, the description, the price, and so on. The actual stock balance is recorded at physical stocktaking and slotted in. This itself might take some time and special procedures will have to be used to keep the balance up to date until live running begins. It is here that parallel running can be very useful. In some systems, however, this direct count of resources is not feasible. When setting up a sales ledger, some companies write to all their customers saying in effect: 'This is what we make your balance as at . . . do you agree?' Small discrepancies are written off and the new file created for live running. (In fact, a little while ago we had a letter from an august computer institution that said they were putting their subscriptions on the computer. It went on to say that the records left something to be desired and could we tell them, please, had we paid?)

The key to successful file conversion is careful planning as early as possible in the project: an agreement of who will do what, how and when. After that management should remember that the best people under stress will undertake more than can be performed.

USER-TRAINING

User staff will have to be trained in the new system. Questions like the following will have to be answered:

— Who will do the training? The Joe-teaches-Bill-teaches-John method rarely works.
— How much of the staff time will be required for training? Will it be during the usual working hours? If so, who will keep the company in business while it's going on?
— What about new staff coming in after the system starts? This is particularly important if you have a high turnover of staff. More than one system has been ruined because the old staff who understood it have left or been promoted, and their replacements never received any proper training.

Again, careful planning as early as possible is the key.

Many companies spend much time and effort explaining to the lower level staff how the new input forms are to be completed. *But don't forget to explain the outputs as well.* One company neglected this aspect of a new system. One very important 'work status report' carried a single date. Various people in the company chased around making different decisions, often conflicting, on the content of this one report. This was all based on different interpretations of the date, among them, for example:

- — date report produced
- — status of work as of . . .
- — cut-off date for the submission of input.

Introducing a new system creates the same problems as any other change: a new manager, a new organization structure, new manual procedures, new manufacturing resources. There will be reaction against the new system if the workers feel that it is being foisted on them without any prior consultation. Add to this a basic mistrust or dislike of computers, and training can be a nightmare. If it proves very difficult to train people in the new system, then this may not just be due to a reaction against the system. Perhaps the system is too complex for them to operate; the forms are too complex, the outputs difficult to interpret and produced at the wrong time. 'Why should we do it this way when the old way was a damn sight easier?' If you have to start modifying a system before it goes into operation because of comments like that, then something was very wrong with the development work. Probably it was a systems analyst who thought more about the machine than the people and a lack of involvement on your part to bring him back into line. To quote from an old manual of seamanship: 'The worst plight in which your ship can be found is to be on a lea shore in a gale. The rules for dealing with this are (1) Never allow your vessel to be in this position.'

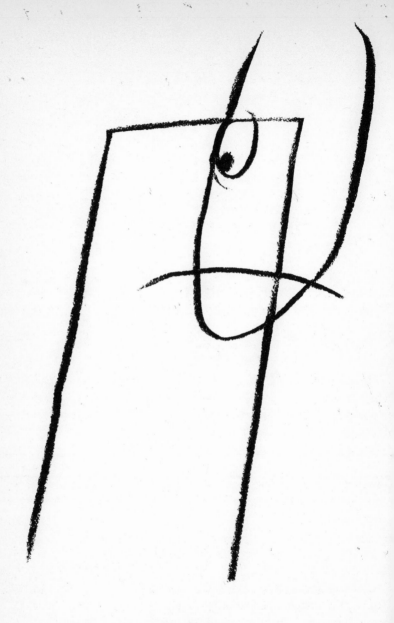

Osborn

15

Just a Little Change

Nothing is permanent, especially when it comes to a computer or computer systems. From the day it begins operating, changes will be required. The possible reasons are:

Previously undetected bugs

These are inevitable. Even if a system has been running smoothly for six years, no experienced computer person would be willing to give a 100 per cent guarantee that no bugs exist. It could be that the particular combination of circumstances that will bring the bug to light just haven't occurred yet. There may be a bug in the year-end routines that takes ten months to show itself. In a new system, bugs are bound to show up for the first few cycles. They have to be fixed immediately; this is 'fireman' maintenance.

Operating efficiency and ease of use

After running and observing the system in live operation a few times, the systems people or the computer operator may be able to suggest some changes to make it run faster and therefore more cheaply. On your side, you may find that the forms and procedures could be improved, in the light of actual practice, to make them easier to use.

Changes in the hardware and/or software

The most radical change would be the acquisition of a new and different computer. Every system in the place has to be completely re-written. This happened to a great many companies with the introduction of the 'third generation' of computers. The new ones were so much bigger and better everybody had to scrap the old ones. Many regretted it. They hadn't realized what a huge job converting all the systems was.* We are now wearier and wiser, and the big step of changing to a new computer is taken reluctantly, if at all. When it is taken, everyone knows how tough it's going to be. More often, there will be a new kind of peripheral, or a new software feature, and it makes sense to change the system to take advantage of it.

Changes in company organization

If departments are re-aligned or an acquisition or merger involving another company takes place, some computer systems may have to be altered to fit.

Changes in company policy

For example, a change in policy to more aggressive selling methods could alter the report requirements in the sales analysis system; changing weekly paid employees to a monthly basis or vice versa would require a re-write of the payroll system; a change in accounting methods could affect almost any system.

* Why didn't they make the new computers compatible with the old ones so you could keep on using your old programs? After a fashion they did, but it didn't work very well and you lost a lot of power on the new machine if you tried to use it that way. That's not a very good answer, but there isn't any better one. It's just another example of the stupidity (or optimism) of some computer people.

Long and short term changes in the business

The addition of a new product line, or dropping old products, could alter the file structures of any system carrying product information; an increase or decrease in volume of business in a particular area could affect almost any system; and so on.

Legal requirements

A new income tax law means that every company with the payroll on the computer has to make changes. Some businesses are more subject to legal reporting requirements than others—banks, insurance companies, and stockbrokers particularly. In Britain, every company with a computer had to change its systems when currency was decimalized a few years ago, and the European Common Market will require more changes, metrication and Value Added Tax not the least among them.

Implementation of related systems

As new systems go on the computer, they may require changes in systems already computerized. To give just one example: if information to feed the inventory control system came straight from the warehouse, when a computerized loading and routing system is installed, the inventory control might have to be changed to get some of its data from the new system instead. Both might have to be changed again when customer ordering is put on.

Each change to an operational system can be classified by its degree of urgency. Emergency requirements come at the top of the list. These can legitimately include bugs and some legal requirements, where not enough notice has been given for the change. On rare occasions, quick changes in the business or in company policy may require panic maintenance, as when the company merges with another and could not make it public in advance. Other changes that become emergencies should not be; they probably started life as short- or long-term requirements,

135

and rose to become panics through mismanagement. Then short-term and long-term changes are required. Most maintenance falls into these categories. It has to be done, but there is ample time to fit it into the regular work schedule.

The last category is desirable but non-essential maintenance. Changes to improve operating efficiency and especially ease of use fall into this category. If you have made a request for such a change (for example, a new report you would like to have but could live without), remember that it costs ten times as much to add it now as it would have done if you had thought of it before programming began. This takes us full circle; try to think of all the things you would like the new system to do during the feasibility study and the detailed information-gathering. Of course, that may be impossible; none of us uses a crystal ball. If you *never* get any of the changes you ask for, or you don't get them without a great deal of grumbling and carrying on from the data processing department, something is wrong down there. They exist to serve you, especially if this work is coming out of your budget. Suggest that when they do some required maintenance, they do your pet changes as well. It's easier and cheaper to do the whole lot at once.

As a final point, you should be aware of how much maintenance costs. In an average company, 40 to 50 per cent of all systems and programming effort is spent on maintenance. The percentage will be higher in companies with many systems computerized. For a new system, estimate that 10 per cent (optimistic) to 20 per cent (conservative) of development costs will be spent on maintenance every year.

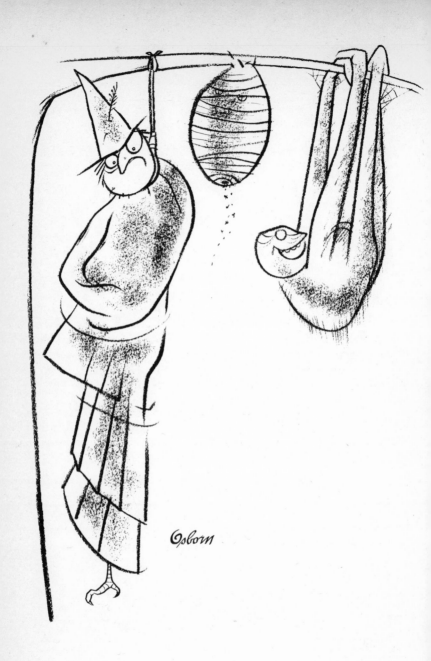

16

Witch-Hunt, Hornet's Nest, and Lethargy

The system is in and running. It may have been delivered on time and on budget. It may have been late and over-cost. You may feel confident, complacent, and pleased. Or you may bitterly regret ever starting the whole project and determined never to do it again. Either way the work is not finished yet.

The next step should be a formal evaluation of the system after it has been running for some time. The amount of time which elapses between the start of live running and the review depends on a number of factors; the most important is the cycle or frequency of the system. If it is a daily system, it could be evaluated after a couple of months; if weekly, after six months, and if monthly or annual, after a year. The requirement is that the system should have been running long enough for its effect to be seen, but not too long for the environment to have changed drastically. If left too long, it may be impossible to differentiate between system errors and changes in the operation of the company. To wait for an annual system to be run three or four times before evaluating it would be ridiculous, for the company would have changed drastically in that time and it would be too late; the damage will have been done. (Many annual systems consist, anyway, of special processing of records which have been created and updated by the daily, weekly, and monthly systems.)

The purposes of the review are to evaluate the operational system against the original objectives and targets, and to investigate whether the system is working well, technically and economically. The benefits of doing a formal review are tremendous, but it is seldom carried out. Why not? Well, there are several possible reasons:

The hornets' nest syndrome

Otherwise known as 'don't disturb the sleeping giant'. 'We went through hell to get that blasted system in. What if it isn't right? You don't mean that we'll have to go through it again? You're joking, of course.'

The witch-hunt syndrome

Otherwise known as 'who wants to stick his neck on the chopping-block?' It's obvious that an evaluation can have two basic verdicts: SUCCESS or FAILURE. What if it is failure? If there is antagonism between user and data processing, or intense internal politics, one group blocks the other to avoid a witch-hunt.

Forward, ever forward

Data processing resources are scarce and the users are busy, so who wants to look back? After all, for the data processing people there are pastures new, and horizons still to be striven for; you are committed one hundred per cent, trying to make the new system work or planning further ambitious projects for your department.

Lethargy

What the hell, anyway.

140

What system?

If the system has been in operation a long time, many changes may have been made and the system modified out of all resemblance to its original form. The business environment and objectives will have changed radically, especially if the system is over five years old. This reason is plausible. But what are you going to do? Continue to hold the system together with string and brown paper until it creaks worse than the one it replaced?

Evaluate against what?

This is perhaps the most damning of all the reasons for not doing an evaluation. There never was a formal, reasoned, quantified user request against which the systems can be tested for success or failure. Of course, it does offer a modicum of job security for all concerned; you'll never be proved wrong.

Assuming an evaluation is done, the answers required from it will vary from job to job and company to company. Here are some examples:

Did we meet the objectives and targets?

This compares the operational system's achievements against its targets, presupposing some form of measurable yardstick such as a user request. *Poor* yardsticks are:

— Original objective was to reduce work in progress in the plant. System has cut work in progress by 0.5 per cent. System=success. Big deal. Perhaps if we'd agreed on a quantified target and looked at other non-computerized possible solutions, things would have been different.
— Original objective was to computerize invoicing. System (invoicing) is on the computer. System=success.
— Original objective was to reduce staff. System resulted in firing Fred (who dropped dead from a heart attack in the panic anyway). System=success.

There are, of course, those systems which are installed as an 'act of faith' because the objectives defy quantifying. But many systems can have quantified objectives and thus can be evaluated, provided the objectives are known.

Have the objectives changed?

The business is dynamic. The objectives and the environment change. How does the new system stand up to these? If the objectives have changed, this will still not rule out the type of review described above.

Does the system work well?

This is a general review of how the system operates, looking at the economic and technical performance in both data processing and user areas.

Were the objectives right in the first place?

This is really one for you. Let's suppose the system has achieved what was wanted. Has it made the impact in costs/revenue/profits that you wanted?

The best type of system in this respect is one which generates regular reports which enable you to monitor the system without setting up a special investigation. Not only should the achievement of the system be compared to objectives, but the development targets (budgets and time-scales) should also be compared to initial estimates. Similarly, operational costs should be matched against original claims.

Be prepared to look for answers in the event of a proven failure: IF NOT, WHY NOT? WHAT DO WE DO ABOUT IT?

This leads us to one of the most important and neglected aspects of the review. It is a learning process. Without the evaluation you will only repeat the mistakes next time.

17

The Jargon Barrier—Phase II

Are you getting hooked on computer jargon yet? Here is a glossary of some more advanced terms.

Algorithm: Any set of rules for performing a certain procedure or calculation. Frequently used because it feels good to say it.

Alphanumeric: A descriptive term applied to data consisting of letters (A to Z), numbers (0 to 9), and/or special characters (+—/@$, etc).

Analog: (British spelling: *analogue*). The representation of numeric quantities by physical means. Mercury thermometers, slide rules, and ordinary clocks are analog devices; so are some special computers used for scientific work.

Assembler: A computer program which takes as input the code written by the programmer, and gives as output instructions the machine can understand. To put it another way, it takes the source program and turns it into object program (qv). Verb: to assemble.

Assembly language: The programming language used with a particular assembler.

Block: A unit of information of convenient size for computer processing. A single record may be too small for efficient reading and writing, so a number of records are blocked together; and as far as the computer is concerned it reads and writes the block as one record.

Branch: In a computer program, to transfer to another instruction which is not necessarily the next one in sequence.

Breakthrough: A solution to a problem which few people realized existed until the computer experts told them about it.

Buffer: A temporary store to equalize two operations of different speeds. Part of the hardware which temporarily holds a record being read in (or written out) of memory, as a wait station. Buffers are necessary because of the differences in speed between the CPU (Central Processing Unit) and various peripheral devices.

Compiler: A program which performs the same functions as an assembler (qv), but for a different type of computer language. Compilers operate on source programs which are written in human-oriented form, mathematical notation, or pseudo-English.

Console typewriter: A typewriter on-line to the computer which allows communication between the machine (via the operating system) and the computer operator. The slowest type of computer device; also considered by some to be the one most likely to go wrong.

Digital: Refers to information represented as numbers; cf analog. All today's business computers are digital.

Direct access: Being able to go directly to a record on computer media without reading preceding records. Disks and memory are direct access devices; magnetic tapes are not.

Field: The smallest meaningful unit of information. What is meaningful in one situation, however, may not be in another. Take the number '4'. If you don't know what it refers to, it doesn't mean anything. Suppose we extend it to: '4 1776'. When that is further expanded to 'July 4 1776', it certainly does mean something to almost everyone; in computer terms, it is now a field.

Similarly, the last half of your bank account number by itself doesn't convey a whole unit of information; the entire number is the field. Your computerized bank record contains a number of fields: account number, name, address, current balance, and so on.

Floating point arithmetic: A way of handling numbers so that any

146

number of decimal point places can be accommodated, without losing accuracy; rounding off to two or three places is not necessary.
Especially important for scientific work.

Interface: Jargoneer's term for any two things, such as computer programs, which act together.

K: a thousand. For example, 100K ch/s=a reading speed of 100,000 characters per second; $15K=salary of analyst $15,000. In American slang K=G.

Key: The field or fields which identify a record. The key for your bank account records at the bank would be the branch number plus your account number: with that knowledge, your account cannot be confused with anybody else's in the whole bank.

Linear programming: Technique for finding an optimum combination, when there may be no single best one. For example, linear programming could be used to solve the problem: 'What combination of foods would give the most calories and best nutrition for the least money?' A computer need not be used; often it is because such problems would take too long to solve by hand.

Macro instruction: A single instruction written by the programmer in a source program (qv), which when assembled results in a series of object instructions for the computer.

Magnetic ink character recognition (MICR): Characters printed in a magnetizable ink, so that they can be read both by human beings and by a special type of computer peripheral. Checks have MICR characters along the bottom. MICR is always pronounced by its initials.

Multiprogramming: Running two or more programs at the same time in the same computer. Most modern computers can do this.

MFT: Multiprogramming with a Fixed number of Tasks, tasks being programs. Also, Multiprogramming with a Finite amount of Trouble.

MVT: Multiprogramming with a Variable number of Tasks. Also, Multiprogramming with a Vast amount of Trouble.

Object program: The instructions which come out of the compiler or assembler, ready to be run on the computer. The object program is the one which is actually run with your data to produce results.

Operand: The part of the computer instruction that specifies *what is to be operated on*. For example, in 'Add 10 to 20', 10 and 20 are operands. (See operation code.)

Operation code: The part of the computer instruction that specifies what type of operation is to be carried out. For example, in 'Add 10 to 20', 'Add' is the operation code.

Optical character recognition (OCR): Characters printed in a special shape so that they can be read both by human beings and by a special type of light-scanning computer peripheral.

Parity bit: An extra bit added to a byte, character, or word, to ensure that there is always either an even number or an odd number of bits, according to the logic of the system. If, through a hardware failure, a bit should be lost, its loss can be detected by checking the parity. The same bit pattern remains as long as the contents of the byte, character, or word remain unchanged.

Real time: No truly satisfactory definition of this term has yet been invented. Usually defined as computer processing for immediate use, or computer operation in a human time-scale. On-line terminals give real time capability.

Sub-routine: A section of code in a program for a particular function.

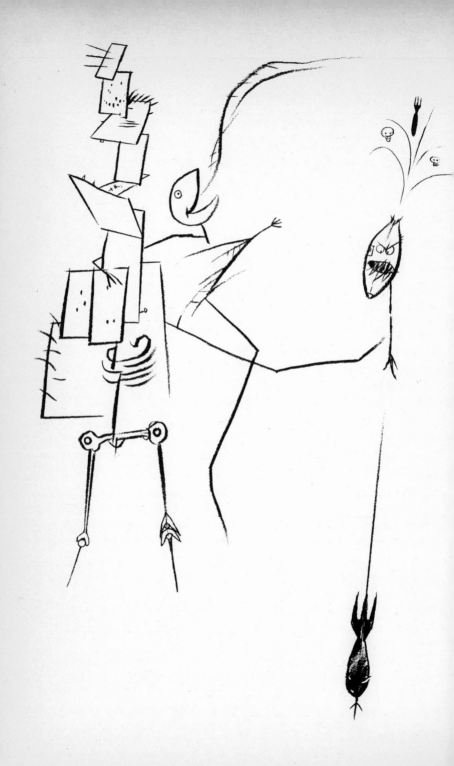

18

Fads, Fancies, and Fantasies

Fashions in data processing come and go like clothing styles. Ideas come into vogue, have their day, and fade away. The speed with which this happens appears to be a direct function of the state of the economy and the profits of the computer manufacturers and consultants. Some ideas get a foothold, are nourished, and stay around for a while in some form or other. This, one supposes, is progress.

Tracing the source of a fad can be like tracing a joke; it seems to have sprung up in half a dozen places at once, and no one can say who thought of it first. But a concept needs support to have a chance. There are computing equivalents of Dior or Chanel—institutions like the Harvard Business School and the Massachusets Institute of Technology (MIT). When one of them puts its weight behind a new idea you can be pretty sure it will be around for a while. The way-out boutiques are the small consultancies, some 'think tanks', and independent technical writers. Some of them can produce an idea which they don't expect anyone to wear for more than six months; that's when it falls apart.

Here are a few examples of ideas which enjoyed great popularity for a while, but have since been buried:

1. *A programming language to produce programs that would work on any computer* without modification. This was, and still

is, a good idea. You wouldn't need to re-program everything if you got a new make of computer; you wouldn't need to change anything if you merged with a company with a different computer. It was killed by two things: nobody could agree on the details, and the computer manufacturers realized that they would sell fewer computers if it really came about.

2. *The concept of magnetic card and magnetic strip storage devices.* The computer records are held on magnetic cards, or strips of tape. These cards or strips hang in the peripheral, and when one is wanted it is flipped out of the stack and brought around to be read juke-box style. (For the technically minded, the biggest were IBM's Data Cell, and RCA's Mass Storage Unit.) In principle this was an excellent idea, because it meant relatively fast access for huge amounts of data; and it was cheap. The drawback was that the devices in operation were subject to frequent mechanical failure. There were too many moving parts. A small handful of companies are still happily using these contraptions. Most found they just couldn't get the blasted things to work.

3. *Critical path networks for managing data processing projects.* The principle of critical path analysis (CPA) is quite simple. A major project is broken down into a number of smaller tasks, called activities. Each activity is given a time (possibly a series of times, from pessimistic to optimistic, together with the resource required). The relationships between the activities are then defined on the basis of 'we can't start this activity before that one is complete, and we can't do that before we've completed these other two tasks', and so on. A network is thus created showing the inter-relationships between the activities. This can then be fed into the computer which analyzes the times and the network pattern and identifies the 'critical path'. The critical path is the series of activities which take the longest time. The entire job cannot be finished before the activities on the critical path have been completed. Special attention can thus be given to these tasks. As other activities slip in time elsewhere in the project, so the critical path can change from week to week.

CPA can only be done without the aid of the computer when the calculations are of a rather simple nature. CPA has been re-invented by every housewife who tries to get all the dishes of a meal hot and on the table at the same time.

This technique of scheduling resources was developed for the Polaris project. It worked beautifully, and has worked well for all kinds of things since, from building spaceships to publishing books. But it didn't work for data processing, except in the very largest installations. The tasks of data processing are not as small and easily definable as those for building a ship.

4. *Automatic debugging:* All that was needed was a high-level compiler that would find all the content errors and most of the logic errors in the program; the programmer only had to correct them. Moreover, the programmer wouldn't have to know what was happening in the computer; this is where 'high-level' came in—the programmer was one level up, away from the machine. Print-outs of what the memory looked like when the program went wrong would no longer be needed. In sum, programming would become a clerical job. Any programmer reading this is probably choking with laughter by now. Twelve years ago it was taken seriously. Theoretically, it might still be possible; its just that no one has been able to produce the compiler to do it.

Some ideas were good, but ahead of their time. They are not completely dead, and may have their day yet; in fact, some have shown definite signs of health lately:

5. *Software packages:* Buying a software package instead of writing the system yourself. On paper this is an excellent idea, with all kinds of advantages; it saves time and money, you need less staff and those you have don't need to be so expert, the software developer has the headaches of maintaining it, and so on. Many people, especially software salesmen, thought this was the greatest thing since sliced bread. Why re-invent the wheel? But unfortunately, a lot of potential buyers could see many reasons for re-inventing the wheel, principally that they wanted their own wheels slightly different from anybody else's; and anyway, why buy it when you can get it free from the

manufacturer, if not this year then next year? But software is getting better, and manufacturers are now making you pay for their software (or the government is making them charge for it, depending on how you look at it). While software has not yet become the boom business many thought it would, more and more installations are taking second looks and re-doing their sums.

6. *The romance of the computer utility*: This means that nobody actually has his own computer; you just have a terminal in your living room, or a few dozen or a few hundred terminals in your offices and factories, and you buy time from a computer center as and when you need it. During the recent business recession, the sound of computer utility companies hitting the dust was thunderous. But the concept is still a good one, and when technology catches up with the romantics you may have that terminal in your home. If not, your children will.

7. *The data base concept*: This one became a fad in the middle '60s, when mass storage of data began to get cheaper. Instead of one system for payroll, one for accounts receivable, one for accounts payable, one for inventory, etc, each with its own set of files (containing some duplicate information), you put all the data together into one set of files, the 'data base'. This would provide a 'pool' of information for use at any particular time. The data files were designed and defined independently of the processing. This idea faded away when people realized how much work it was going to be. They were barely keeping their heads above water with the old approach; this one would cost more and take longer. Better the devil you know than the devil you don't. Nowadays, companies who are getting their data processing management straightened out and their old systems working smoothly are again beginning to look at the data base idea, but more realistically.

8. *Management information systems* (MIS): The sophisticated MIS are related to the data base concept. Your computer should not just be doing the clerical drudgery, it should be producing information for management decision-making and even making the decisions. After all, computers are so much more dispassionate

than humans; why trust your decision-making to fallible, emotional people? The principle is like this; you put all your data into a large pot. This is the data base. Then you light a fire under it. That is the programs. Whatever boils over the top is management information. One large bank tried it, and they put a television screen on the president's desk. At any time he could push a button and see the assets of the bank displayed, up to the minute and correct to the nearest penny. Management information—great. The bank spent a round million getting the system installed, and the president sat down at his desk to look at his television screen and push his little button. And you know what? He couldn't think of a single reason *why* he needed to know the total assets of the bank, up to the minute and correct to the nearest penny.

A good management information system has to be built on a foundation of good record-keeping. They're expensive and take time to develop properly. Gone about sensibly, an MIS can be a real benefit to a company.

9. *User programming*: Why should systems analysts and programmers be placed between the user and the computer? Why shouldn't the *user* write his own programs to produce his special or one-off reports? It's a very nice concept. It would certainly be welcomed by the data processing people, to whom small programs for special reports can be an irksome chore, interrupting their main development work. This approach requires the use of very simple, high-level languages. It also requires the use of a data base which can be easily manipulated by the user. One technique is to use a special set of software programs called a *generalized file processor*. An example of this type of software is Informatic's MARK IV, one of the most famous and successful packages. This is a type of data base management system which, according to a trade catalog, 'normally results in a 10 to 1, or greater reduction, over conventional programming languages . . .'

10. *Modular programming*: This is an example of a technique that many people were using before it was formally christened and launched as a 'new concept'. As described in Chapter 12, a

commercial program can consist of a thousand or more coded instructions. Modular programming is based on the old axiom 'divide and rule'. Rather than designing, coding, and testing one large program, it is broken down into a number of small, easy-to-manage, modules. Each module is a logical unit which does one major task (such as read and check input), performs one type of calculation (such as special discount rates), or produces one type of report entry. Each module is prepared *and tested* individually. They are then put together to form the completed program which is tested as a whole. The advantages claimed: better management control of programming, the ability to split a program among a number of programmers, and, generally, better quality programs.

11. *Decision tables*: What complicates the development of a computer system (and generally makes business systems difficult) is *conditional logic*, where different actions are taken in different conditions. You can see and hear this if you talk to a clerk or the chief executive, or read any procedure manual. In narrative it comes in the form of 'If . . . then . . .', 'but', with linkages like 'and', 'however', 'notwithstanding', and so on. For example, 'if it's a works order for an export customer, and it has a low priority, but is in an credit-assisted area but not in the Eastern bloc, then . . .' The standard technique is to use a flowchart to show conditional logic as described on pages 96–7. Decision tables are another way of showing conditional logic.

Rule 1 of the chart is read as 'If the employee is classed as works and has worked more than 40 hours, pay him his basic rate plus overtime.' Rule 5: 'If the employee is classed as staff and has worked more than 40 hours and has a salary of at least $9000, pay him basic only.' See page 142.

It's a very simple and elegant way of showing complex logic, and is being increasingly used by data processing people.

12. *Telecommunications*: Otherwise known as TP (tele-processing). This is the technique of transmitting data over lines, such as public or private telephone lines. This means that small input/output units in outlying branch offices can be on-line to a central computer at the head office; or that computers at regional

offices can be linked together, and so on. The link can be between cities, states, countries, or even continents. It has resulted in considerable centralization of computer hardware in large companies; local computers have been replaced with terminals on-line to a big central computer. TP has had a checkered career. It depends on the availability of reliable and fast data transmission lines. In most countries this is the responsibility of a monopoly or near-monopoly (government-controlled in some instances) which has not lived up to the demands of the users or the computer manufacturers.

CONDITIONS: what determines the action to be taken

Header: title of the decision-making procedure shown (in this case the policy for making overtime payments to different grades of employees)

TIME PAYMENTS	1	2	3	4	5	6	7	8
Personnel class:	WORKS	WORKS	WORKS	STAFF	STAFF	STAFF	STAFF	EXEC-UTIVE
Hours worked:	>40	=40	<40	=40	>40	>40	<40	-
Salary > $9,000?	-	-	-	-	Y	N	-	-
PAY BASE	X	X		X	X	X		X
PAY BASE + OVERTIME	X					X		
PRODUCE ABSENCE REPORT			X				X	

actions: what is to be done

- indifferent   < less than
> greater than   Y yes
= equals   N no
X take action

rules: the actions to be taken for a particular combination of conditions

157

19

Fingers O'Flaherty and Other Villains

Do you have a computer system that takes as input suppliers' invoices and writes out the checks for them? If you do, somebody may be defrauding the company at this very moment. It's easy. Let's say you've got a dishonest systems analyst, one Fingers O'Flaherty. He makes up a phoney invoice, perhaps from his brother-in-law's company, and puts it into the pile of invoices waiting to be keypunched for the computer system. Or he makes his own punched card with the appropriate information on it, and puts it into the deck of cards along with all the others. It goes through the system, a check is printed and is signed along with hundreds of others; perhaps pre-signed checks are used. Who is to know it's not a legitimate invoice? Exactly this type of fraud is reported in the newspapers on average about once every six months. We don't know how many aren't reported, nor how many are still going on that haven't been discovered. Ah, you say, there are dozens of ways to stop that fiddle. Yes, but is *your* company using them?

There are hundreds of other true cases like this; many companies have had Fingers O'Flahertys. For example:

— The programmer in a bank whose program calculated

savings account interest; instead of dropping off fractions of pennies, he added them to his own account. Everything balanced. He is now alive and rich and living in Rio.

— The programmer for a payroll system who chopped a few cents off each pay check and added them to his own. Again, everything balanced. He was not so lucky; he is now alive and poor and living in the state penitentiary.

— The two young girl clerks in a bank who worked for the section that handled mutilated checks. They deliberately mutilated their *own* checks so the computer would reject them. When they got them back, they literally threw them away. The fraud amounted to about $1500 by the time they were inevitably caught because the bank's accounts wouldn't balance. A court fined them $150 and let them go. Not a bad return on investment.

— Another payroll programmer put a sub-routine in to check for his own final salary check. When the program found it, it automatically moved the decimal point over to the right and added zeroes. This one *didn't* balance, but by the time someone got around to reading the report he had cashed the check and disappeared.

— A very elegant fraud was committed by two systems analysts who worked for a company that imported and exported metal ores. They set up their *own* company that bought from and sold to their employer. Fine; except that they bought at a lower price than they sold. It was all done through the computer system, which they controlled. They were eventually discovered and fired; they kept their company and are still in business. Honestly, one hopes.

— An outside consultant who found a blank form used for adding a new employee to the company payroll. He used it to add himself. Since he was doing a six-month study in the computer department, he could just pick up his check as it came off the computer. (They were pre-signed.)

— The army programmer who set up an entire imaginary base, with 200 men on it. He opened 200 bank accounts for their pay checks. Only after he had the whole thing working well did the awful truth dawn: he would never be caught *as long as he kept it up*. The army never questions an extra 200 men, but there certainly would be questions if they all suddenly disappeared. He considered having them desert *en masse*, dropping an imaginary bomb on the base, having them wiped out by an imaginary case of food poisoning, and finally gave himself up in despair.

Fingers O'Flaherty can be more destructive than this. Master files in particular are at risk because they contain so much information in such a small space. For example:

— One of the easiest routines to put in a program is one that simply wipes out the files. For example, in a payroll system the programmer checks to see if he is still on payroll every month. If he isn't . . .

— Remember that computer files are on magnetic media. A powerful magnet anywhere near them, or a small toy magnet held close, will scramble the data so it's useless.

— Ransom is a possibility too. In this case Fingers O'Flaherty was a computer operator who didn't show up for work on Monday morning. A few days later the company had a long-distance phone call from him; he was in an unnamed European city. He told them he had with him the only copy of one of their master files. They checked; he was right. He demanded, for its return, that they deposit the equivalent of $25,000 in a numbered Swiss bank account. The company paid. It might have been your company and your file.

You may be at risk, too, if your system has confidential data that you wouldn't like to fall in the hands of a competitor, supplier, or even your rival in the next department.

— One company put in a new computer system to plan salesman's calls. Each week it gave each salesman a list of customers to visit, including what they usually bought, what discounts they got, and so on. A good idea? Their competitor thought so, too. Every time a salesman made a call, he found that the competition had just been there and had given the customer a slightly better price. Fingers O'Flaherty was a computer operator who was selling the competitor an extra copy of the customer list.

— A programmer at a major oil company was fired. He got hold of a computer terminal and was able to dial through the public telephone system and get connected with his ex-employer's computer. (This was possible because he knew all the right codes.) He was discovered, but the company is still wondering what he planned to do with all the confidential financial data he was milking out of the computer.

— Programs are valuable too. One company put thousands into developing a program to optimize truck routes. It worked, too; they were able to do the same number of deliveries with 25 per cent fewer trucks. The programmer quit, and went into business for himself selling a transport optimization system. The company knew they should have been getting those profits, but they couldn't prove it.

Below is a comprehensive list of the kinds of problems that come under the general heading of 'security'. The first two have already been discussed.

1. *Fraud*
2. *Confidential data* (including programs).
3. *Theft*—Not only of files, but of the computer equipment itself.

4. *Accidental damage*—This includes fire, flood, explosion, hurricanes, and other Acts of God, as well as human errors.

5. *Civil disturbance*—The risk depends on the location of the building and type of business. Companies unpopular with activist groups because of their policies or products are particularly at risk, as are those in areas where riots are likely to occur. Almost anyone may be the victim of a bomb scare, real or hoax, these days.

6. *Deliberate damage to equipment or files* by a disgruntled or unbalanced employee or outsider.

7. *Erroneous input*, especially if it is not detected and thrown out by the system. If the errors are subtle, it can be months before you discover that something is wrong—maybe never.

8. *Undetected bugs*—Never assume that any system is completely debugged. (See Chapter 12.)

9. *Hardware and software failures* that damage files and data. Power cuts are included in this category—more of a problem in some parts of the world than in others.

We hope we have you thoroughly worried by now. The first step in protecting yourself is to be aware of the risks. A little imagination and thought will enable you to figure out where your own systems may be most at risk. Work with the data processing department to identify the risks, the likelihood of a security break occurring, and the cost of protection. Some risks, obviously, are so unlikely that protective measures are not worthwhile. For example, if your computer is in New York City, you don't need to worry about earthquakes; on the West Coast, this is a real concern for companies with computers. Similarly, if your computer system has nothing to do with accounting or money, the possibility of a fraud is remote.

If you are given a computer-based system to review, look at it and ask yourself: 'WHAT IF . . .' Then see if the systems analyst has thought of it.

Here is a checklist of the kinds of things you, together with the data processing department, can do. It is set out in chart form to indicate the areas of responsibility in each.

Security responsibilities

Procedure	Overall responsibility	Carried out by
file back-up and recovery	user departments	data processing
input control and correction	user departments	data preparation and user department
programmed controls —financial systems	company accounts and auditors	systems and programming
programmed controls —other systems	user department	systems and programming
control of access to building	top management	top management and security guards
control of access to computer area	data processing	data processing and security guards
fire detection	top management	data processing
fire prevention	top management	data processing
evacuation of computer area due to fire, bomb, or other emergency	top management	data processing
prevent unauthorized changes to programs	data processing and company accountants and auditors	data processing
control access to confidential information	top management and user departments	data processing and user departments
checking data processing personnel	top management	personnel department and/or data processing

Procedure	Overall responsibility	Carried out by
safeguard system documentation	data processing	data processing
control program library	data processing	data processing
terminal security for on-line systems	all	user departments and data processing
preparing and updating security standards	top management	data processing
review security	all	top management and/or data processing

20

If It Can Go Wrong It Will

This chapter is about failure. Specifically, it is about why computer systems go wrong. For many years it has been our hobby to analyze the reasons why computer systems fail. Some of the more spectacular ones have been widely reported in the trade press and even in daily newspapers. In a number of cases we were called in as consultants to help clear up the mess afterward. In a few, we were ourselves connected with the project, and we took particular care to analyze the causes of failure in those. What we have found is that the reason always comes under one of these three headings:

— failure to set firm objectives at the start
— failure to involve the user from the start
— too much concern with the computer and not enough with people

Failure to set firm objectives at the start: The importance of setting specific objectives for a computer project has been emphasized in previous chapters. To repeat briefly: If you don't set clear, quantified objectives at the beginning, you have nothing to aim for while designing the system, and when it's finished you won't even know if it's what you wanted. One of our client companies called us in a few months ago to help them settle an internal dispute. We didn't know what the argument was, or who was on which side. The manager started off by telling us he wanted us to do an evaluation of a new payroll system that had just been computerized. We asked to see the user request and the feasibility study. In each one, the only objective stated was 'computerize the payroll'.

'Right,' we said.

'Do you have a computer?'

'Yes, it's just down the hall there.'

'Is the payroll system running on it?'

'Yes.'

'Then you were successful in meeting your objectives.'

And we sent him a bill for evaluating the system. That was the only evaluation possible under the circumstances; yes, we could have looked at operator's logs, console logs, and error reports and worked out how much it was costing to run, and so on and so on, but it wouldn't have told us anything because there was nothing to compare with, no estimated costs, no expected benefits, nothing. The company was still left with many people who were unhappy with the computer system. We recommended they go back to the start and try to establish exactly what they wanted the system to do; *then* they could tell who was justified in complaining and who was not, and decide what changes were needed.

Failure to involve the user from the start: This has got many systems into trouble, but it isn't as easy to spot as late equipment or failure to establish firm objectives. The user just doesn't get involved and the systems development project goes on around him. For example, the user manager has no contact with the project until a checkpoint arrives when a bulky report drops on his desk 'for approval'. Either the user reads it carefully (to cries of delay from the data processing side) or skims through it and signs on the dotted line. Ah, ah, cry the data processing people, savouring the signature, he's signed for it. The project goes on, and then, of course, the alterations and changes come to light, and no amount of whining from the computer people that 'he signed for it' will get that project back on time. So one effect on that project would be maintenance work before the system is even in.

Another area where lack of user involvement really puts a project back is in the latter stages of testing, conversion, and implementation. 'Oh no,' says the user, 'the computer people can convert that file and train those people. After all, it is their system. They can't just develop it and leave the dirty work to us.' Or after the fourth month of systems testing or at the start of the second year's parallel running, the user still isn't prepared to accept the system for live running.

User involvement does take time and effort. But it's the only way to get a system that you want and can use, on time.

Too much concern with the computer and not enough with people: This is a direct result of the fact that systems are designed by technicians, especially ex-programmers, who are oriented toward the computer and have no outside business experience. The systems they design are wonderfully efficient on the machine and hell for the people who supply the input and use the output.

There are three basic sub-divisions in this category:

Lack of attention to the input side: A large publishing company put in a new computer system to process orders. The systems people re-designed the order form that the salesmen had to fill in, to make it easy to get the orders into the computer. Unfortunately, they never considered the poor salesmen; the form was practically impossible to fill in quickly under field conditions, taking orders from busy book-store managers. Unbeknown to the computer people, the sales manager hired a large group of clerks. The salesmen continued to use their old forms and the clerks copied it all out by hand onto the new forms for the computer. The extra work almost doubled the true running cost of the system. When we were called in to find out why it was costing so much, we found that roomful of clerks. The answer was simple: re-design the order form so it was easy to fill in *and* nice for the computer. This problem was, of course, compounded by the lack of communication between the user and the data processing department.

Lack of attention to the output side: An electronics firm wished to improve their cash flow by getting invoices out sooner. Under the old system, invoices were prepared by hand and were sent out as much as two months late. They put in a computer system which printed all the month's invoices on the last day of the month. Theoretically, this would improve the situation to the point where no invoice would be more than a month behind, and the average delay would be only two weeks. Fine. The first month, the invoices came rolling off the computer all correct; it took about a half hour to print them. The systems analyst then went away whistling to start another project. But the company's cash flow did not improve at all. Some months later there was an investigation. They found one poor little man in the mail room. Under the old system, he got the invoices in dribs and drabs all month, and got them out the best he could. Under the new system, he got all the invoices on the same day. It took him a month to fold them, put them in envelopes, address them, stamp them, and send them out. The systems people had given no thought to what would happen to the output after it came off the computer; they never identified the bottleneck in the mail room. As a result, the new system accomplished nothing at all.

The blinker effect: No computer system can operate in splendid isolation. It affects and is affected by other systems and a wide variety of business conditions. The impact that a new system makes can go beyond the obvious things that were expected. If the systems people have not thought through all the implications, if they have been looking only straight ahead, the results can be disastrous.

A wholesaler put in a computerized inventory and customer ordering system. During the investigation stage, the systems analysts discovered that each customer ordered, on the average, once every three months. The objectives of the new system were to reduce out-of-stocks and process the orders faster. They succeeded admirably; out-of-stocks were reduced by a significant proportion, and the customers got their goods much faster than before. That pleased the customers, of course. Under the old system they had had to order way ahead to be sure of getting what they wanted in time, because of delays and out-of-stocks. Now they didn't need to, and they changed their ordering pattern. Instead of ordering once every three months, they did it once a month. The average order was one third the size of an old one, so it didn't mean any extra business for the wholesaler. But he had three times as many orders to process, three times the paperwork to do. The computer system wasn't built to handle this volume and it rapidly broke down.

This is a more subtle kind of problem than the two previous examples. A typical systems analyst anywhere could have easily missed seeing the possible results. Realizing what was going to happen, and taking steps to avoid it or cater for it, takes imagination, a thorough understanding of the company's business and good communications with management. Systems analysts who wear blinkers and see only straight ahead will fall into traps like this time after time.

There are, of course, other problems that can occur during the course of a project. They may result in delay or even the need to modify the objectives. But by themselves they do not necessarily guarantee failure of the system. The factors we have discussed will always do so.

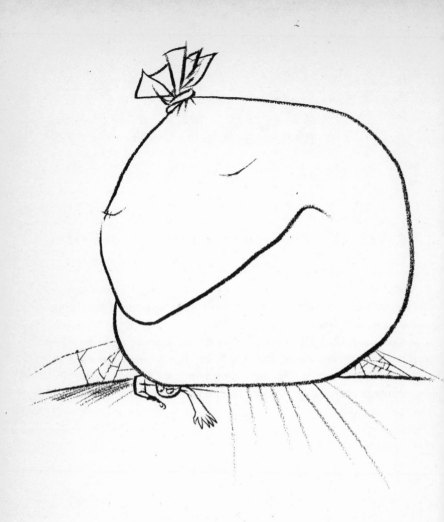

21

Everything Takes Longer and Costs More

The fact that everything takes longer and costs more is not limited to data processing projects. The maxim can usually be applied to public works, for example: a new bridge that costs twice as much as the original estimates; an airport that keeps getting postponed because it's so expensive, and eventually has to be built at three times its cost ten years ago; a power plant that is three years late going into operation. The rule also applies to almost any high-technology project from a new type of supersonic aircraft to the channel tunnel between England and France. That one has been delayed for over a hundred years now.

We were talking to a large group of production, research, and development users in a large electronics company. They were bemoaning the fact that nearly all computer systems were over-budget and late. We'd expected this one and had done our home-work. 'How many of *your* new products and processes', we asked, 'go in on time, on budget, according to initial estimates?' Silence. It's no excuse; data processing should be better than everyone else, but it isn't.

Management of data processing departments in business organizations has always been particularly poor. There are, of course, exceptions; a few companies have very good computer management. Many do not. There are a number of reasons for his, connected with the history of computers in business.

In their early days, management of computers was in the hands of mathematicians and engineers. The first big companies to use computers required all programmers to have a degree in mathematics; they had to, because programming was so difficult in those days. The academic tradition was reinforced by the fact that most early computers were built at universities or research laboratories connected with universities. The only people who had real experience with computers were academics, and this carried over into business. The people who ran the computers were professors, PHDs, mathematicians and engineers, none of whom are ever expected to have a 'head for business' or be concerned about costs and profits. (This tradition still exists very strongly on most campuses today. The authors recently met a college professor who was in charge of the school computer center. He had tried to set it up as a profit-making organization by selling the extra computer time to nearby businesses, a move that would be approved by any hard-headed business man. The poor professor, however, was ostracized by his colleagues; old friends cut him dead on the campus, and he became a *persona non grata*, a social pariah. As he explained it to us, 'management' and 'profit' were dirty words; he was lowering himself and disgracing his profession by talking about them.) And so a hangover from those early days sometimes exists in business today—the feeling that it is a little gauche to ask the computer people to be concerned about budgets and timetables; their minds are on loftier things. Computer people have been known to encourage this attitude, of course.

Another factor is the rapid growth of data processing in business. For years, an acute shortage of trained people existed. Standards for hiring programmers, for example, dropped rapidly; there just weren't enough people with degrees in mathematics to fill a fraction of the jobs open. The development of high-level programming languages, which made the job less technical, helped. The law of supply and demand operated; there were many more jobs than people to fill them, and salaries rocketed. It was a young person's profession; in many companies, the average age in the data processing department was the early twenties, even taking the managers into account. Promotion was rapid. The traditional career path was, and to a large extent still is, programmer to systems analyst to manager. It was not unusual for a young man to start as a programmer straight out of college and within six or seven years to be managing an entire data processing department of fifty, sixty or more people.

Consider the effect: the entire department staffed by young people without business experience and maturity, people who had no work experience in any other area of business; moreover, people who had salaries much higher than those of their counterparts in other departments. If they weren't happy, or wanted more money, changing jobs was easy. At the peak of the boom, the programmer stayed on average less than two years. Coupled with fast promotion and high staff turnover was the 'promoted technician syndrome'. The best programmers soon became systems analysts; the top systems analyst was promoted to be data processing manager. In each case, the skills required for the job were entirely different from those needed in the previous job. A good programmer may make a bad systems analyst, and a skilled analyst may be the world's worst manager. Many of them were.

It is no wonder that data processing developed a reputation for poor management, missed deadlines, and mushrooming budgets.*

Too much optimism is probably the most common immediate cause of these problems. Almost everyone in data processing seems to suffer from it, including consultants, software houses, and computer manufacturers.

One of the worst cases we have seen in recent years was at an international insurance company. The company had a number of computer installations around the world, so one would have

---

* We were very impressed when a data processing manager told us that, in his installation, he always kept to his schedules and budgets. Talking to his staff later, we discovered they were revised from week to week, until the final target was set in the last week of the project.

thought they would have learned from experience. Not so. They planned an international telecommunications network, with offices in half a dozen countries feeding information into a central computer complex for processing. The major tasks included selecting, ordering, and installing equipment, getting the central computer installed and working, hiring systems analysts and programmers, designing the system, and programming and training staff in half a dozen different languages: all of which would have been reasonable if they set it up as a five- or six-year project. But they planned to do it all in *less than a year*. The senior management of the company were so impressed—or stunned—that they okayed the project. A year later the equipment hadn't been installed, the systems hadn't been designed, and not all the programmers had been found. They had barely started. At this point senior management woke up, cancelled the whole project, and fired everybody connected with it. Upward of half a million dollars had been thrown away, much of it on international travel for the project managers.

Why did this project ever get approved with a timetable like that? The only answer is incredible over-optimism on the part of the people who planned it, along with awed naïvete from senior management, who (for a time at least) believed everything they were told. Any experienced outsider, not emotionally committed to the project, could have told them it was ridiculous. Which is what we did, in the early days. We were quietly invited to peddle our goods elsewhere, but we had the dubious satisfaction of seeing our predictions come true a year later.

Most missed deadlines do not occur on so grand a scale. The over-optimism is usually not so much in over-estimating how much work can be done in a given time period, but in forgetting that certain tasks have to be done, and in forgetting that things will go wrong.

Almost every medium- to large-scale computer project these days is skirting the edges of the unknown, at least as far as the people on the project are concerned. They've never done anything really like this before. Technology is advancing daily, there will be new types of equipment, new software, new techniques. In such situations, it is essential to build into the timetable, and the budget, a contingency factor. Things will go wrong. That is a dead certainty. Unfortunately, it is not possible to predict in advance exactly *what* things will go wrong. It's like an insurance company's actuarial tables. They show that, given a group of people of a certain age, a certain percentage of them will die in a given time period. It is absolutely impossible to predict *who* will die, but you can bet that a certain number will.

On a computer project planned to take several years, it is a certainty that some of the staff will quit, be fired, or be taken ill, that the equipment will break down, that the requirements will be changed in the middle of the project, that a supplier will be late with equipment or software, that a program will turn out to be more complicated than anyone thought, that the company's business will change in some way, that new management with different ideas will come in . . . and/or a dozen other possibilities. You can't tell in advance which of these will happen, but some of them are sure to. The only way to plan for them is to build some slack into the plans, to allow for something going wrong, even if you don't know what it will be. This is a lesson that computer people always have to learn the hard way.

The blame does not lie entirely with the computer people; top management is at fault too. They allowed themselves to be blinded with science, they were too lazy to learn new concepts to understand what was going on. They put increasing pressure on the computer people to get the systems running, hire more people, expand the department, use the computer more—without considering what it was costing or what troubles they were storing up for the future. Lower-level management is also culpable when they don't review data processing reports at checkpoints.

The battle is half won if you realize that everything *does* take longer and cost more. You can then view the over-optimistic plans of the computer people in the proper light, carry out the necessary changes, and make your own plans for what to do when things go wrong.

22

When the Fit Hits the Shan

This chapter is about what to do when a computer system goes sour. That doesn't mean that you should expect a computer system to collapse; but it is a fact that some do. In some companies almost all the systems are abject failures. With careful planning and hard work it is possible to produce a system which at least holds its own or is even of definite benefit to the company. In previous chapters, we give guidelines for doing it. But supposing you are faced with a calamity as a *fait accompli*?

Before we answer that, let's look at the three major categories of bad systems:

1. *It costs more to operate the new computer than the old one, with no matching benefits*. Expenses rocket while revenue rises only marginally, stays constant, or, if you're really in trouble, falls. For example, one company put in an inventory control system to monitor stock levels and to reduce the capital tied up in stocks, while maintaining good customer service. Additional data was collected from the salesmen and the warehouse, the computer carried out complicated and time-consuming analysis, and massive reports were produced. The new system was approximately five times more expensive than the original stock control system. It did not make any sizeable impact on the capital tied up in stocks, nor any improvement in customer service. Reasons: the input

information was suspect, computer processing was badly designed, and the output reports were not in the right format. *Result*: money going down the drain.

In another company, a sophisticated (and costly) management reporting system was installed, producing reports on many aspects of the company's activities. The reports did not contain accurate or current information, with the result that they were not used by the management. *Result*: an expensive system without matching benefits. It was eventually thrown out, and the costs written off.

In the case of the inventory control system, no actual damage was done to the stock-on-hand position or to customer service. It just didn't do what it was supposed to do, and it ate money. In the management reporting example, the company was acually paying to be deprived of information they used to get.

2. *There is a combination of minor irritants and confusions which, taken together, lead to a general falling off of efficiency and effectiveness.* This is the case where it isn't possible to point directly to one major failure in the system. For example, in one system, a company suffered from the following:

— the system wasn't ready when a new range of products was to be released and a temporary system had to be used.

— the processing programs contained errors of logic which led to late reports, and users spent considerable time debugging the output data.

— users mistrusted parts of the system to the extent that they kept their own manual files (a considerable duplication of effort).

— time spent on completing input forms was excessive, to the detriment of actually getting things done.

Most of the data processing people who had installed the system left for greener pastures; of those who remained, no one wanted to be associated with the 'problem system'. *Result*: the users were stuck with it. They still are, as far as we know.

3. *The system results in the gross misuse of the company's*

resources or seriously damages the trading position. This is a true disaster and is easier to see than the situations described above. The mechanics of the computer system are usually blamed, but it may be management's fault. One company we know installed a sales forecasting system which produced accurate and timely reports, including sales projections. Management had approved the system, which was very expensive, because of hard selling by the computer technicians. Management, enamoured with the apparent scope and completeness of the reports, neglected to take into account external factors operating in the market. These, of course, were not shown in the internally generated reports. Economic trends, what the competition was doing, impending social legislation, all were ignored. The company went into liquidation about a year after the system was implemented.

In another case, a new order processing/invoicing system was implemented. The work was done too fast, and the system contained many errors when it began to operate on real data. There was a drastic fall in customer service and, soon after, in sales. The company subsequently sold out to one of its competitors at a bargain basement price.

One of the most interesting—and saddest—questions we're asked is: 'I have this system, *they* put it in a year ago, and it's a real disaster. What do I do?'

The first rule is: *don't panic*, no matter how great the disaster appears to be. It's probably taken two or three years to get this bad and nothing you can do in a week or two is likely to change it. A rescue operation which seeks to solve the immediate crisis can make a harsher rod to beat your back in the future.

Don't throw good money after bad. There will be probably more work in the pipeline: *stop it.* The data processing manager may want to improve things by enlarging the system, and getting a bigger computer. The enhanced system will not only solve the immediate problems but will reap greater benefits which, of course, will pay for the inadequacies (mistakes) in the current system. Like hell it will. It is surprising how many companies do this. It won't solve your problems; it will generate bigger ones.

Now, some alternatives for cleaning up the mess. While you can't make everything sweet overnight, changes can be made in a matter of weeks or months.

Go back to manual methods: This will be possible only if

— the change-over to a computer was fairly recent, and
— you have (or can afford to get) the staff to do it, and
— it is technologically possible; you can't put a man on the moon with slide rules and adding machines.

Whether you consider this a temporary solution until the computer system can be fixed, or you've decided to have nothing to do with computers from now on under any circumstances, going back to the old way of doing things, if it is at all possible, should be seriously considered. We were talking to a senior manager in a life insurance company recently. 'What I'd really like to do', he said, 'is to get rid of the computer and hire a thousand clerks with quill pens. But even if we could afford it, there aren't that many good clerks looking for jobs.' You may be luckier, especially if your people have not yet been absorbed into other parts of the company. Get them back, get the computer records printed out, put in some overtime to correct them, and Bob's your uncle, you're back in business.

But you may find that you are too firmly locked in to the computer system to break away. Some other possibilities are:

Make a real stink: Get top management concerned, and insist that the computer people concentrate their resources on sorting out the problems with the system before going on to anything new. It may be expensive, but cheaper than limping along with a system that only half works.

Use a service bureau: A service bureau is a company that specializes in running other people's systems. They have their own computer, and you can buy its time by the hour. Most service bureaus have a set of packaged systems for standard types of work like payroll, sales analysis, mailing lists. If your system is a fairly standard one, you can probably find a service bureau with a package to do it for you. The advantages are that the system is ready and working, and that you can easily calculate your costs in advance, either in terms of hours of computer time or on a unit basis—so many pay checks printed, for example. The disadvantage is that their package may not do exactly what you want, but for a temporary solution, it's better than nothing at all. Have your legal people review the contract to be sure you don't have to pay if they don't produce.

Here are two suggestions for a more lasting solution:

Consider facilities management: This is a longer-term solution. All systems development and operational work is sub-contracted to an outside organization, who run the department on your premises. You are an expert on making widgets, publishing books, or selling refrigerators; let computer experts run the computer. You pay a fixed annual fee to the facilities management people; the fee will probably be less than the department is costing now. They make their profit by doing the work more efficiently.

Make the data processing department a cost center: Again, this is a long-term solution and can't help you through the immediate crisis. For every job, the data processing department has to submit a bid; you say yes or no. Experience has shown that companies who operate this way have more success with computer systems than those who don't. If you agree to let them do the work, they must do it for that price. If they miscalculate, they have to find the money somewhere else. If they consistently miscalculate, the department will run itself into the ground. But before this happens the manager and his senior staff will be out looking for other jobs, and the company can hire better people.

We hope you never have to turn to this chapter with sweating palms. We believe that, if you follow the advice in other parts of the handbook, you will never need to. The best way to recover from a disaster is not to let it happen in the first place.

23

A Dozen Embarrassing Questions to Ask the Computer Manager

Throughout this book, we have talked about how and why things can go wrong in a computer project. Today, the situation is beginning to change. Too many companies have lost too much money on their computers. The computer people are being required to produce and stick to budgets and schedules, just like any other department in the company. An indication of the trend is the changing career path; systems analysts are now not always ex-programmers, but are brought in from other departments in the company. Some brave companies are even putting in new data processing managers, taken from other areas in the company; they are not ex-programmers and ex-systems analysts, but ex-production control managers, ex-accountants. These new managers may have a rough time at first until they gain the grudging respect of the computer technicians, but they are *managers*. Another indication of the trend is that the technicians are being required to learn something about *business*. They are sent on general business courses, they serve apprenticeships in other departments. They are at last beginning to learn that the company is in business to make a profit, and that the sole purpose of the computer is to help toward that end. The data processing department is beginning to *use* systems as well as *sell* them.

But there is still a long way to go in many companies. Attitudes change slowly. The computer people have a long history to overcome. The department managers whose systems are put on the computer have a responsibility to insist that the development and management of their system is done in a business-like way, with concern for costs and timetables.

The objective of this chapter is to provide you with a list of important points for ensuring that your data processing people are providing you with the best possible service. Some are fundamental to the management of the department, and some minor— but ask the questions so that they will show *you* are concerned and on the ball. They are called 'embarrassing questions' because they cover the areas in which data processing management is still the weakest in many companies. There is a baker's dozen of them, divided into two groups. The first are ones to ask when they are planning a new system for you.

1 *Can you get somebody else to do the work?*

In most companies this question will cause widespread consternation. When you're going to buy a new car, you can shop around for the best deal; why can't you shop around for the best computer system? Maybe you could get the work done faster and/or cheaper by going outside the company. There are dozens of software and programming companies that would be delighted to prove they can. If company policy insists that the data-processing department is a monopoly, then ask them to prove they can do the work economically.

2 *May I see the project plan and schedule?*

In other words, their proposed method of going about the project, and the timetable for it. If they don't have one you would be foolish to authorize the work; there will be no way to control the time and money spent on it. You are giving them a blank check.

If a project plan *is* produced, then ask, as pleasantly as possible, the basis for the time/resource estimates. Of course you can't argue points of technical detail—just try to get a feel of how the estimates are arrived at. One of the most likely replies is 'It's experience, you know'. If you get that, enquire pointedly how accurate the estimates were on previous projects. (It's pretty easy to check this out with other users.) If they were wrong on those, they will give a thousand and one reasons why exceptional conditions cause the delay. Ask what makes this estimate any different. Any good computer manager worth his salt will, by this time, be explaining that all the delays were caused by the short-comings of the users. Don't be put off by this one, ask what they were. Then point out, still politely, that this is very interesting; where on the project schedule is a list of the things that you have to do and how long will it take? Then smile and say: 'Fine, if we do our bit, there's no reason why the project shouldn't come in on time, is there?' If in answer to the original question he produces a list of time-charts, standard formulae and so on, ask pointedly if you will be paying for the time that the analysts spend keeping this mumbo-jumbo up-to-date? Will the project team spend more time writing up their progress on time-forms than working? Then revert to the question sequence given above. You're not being nasty (not much anyway), but you must be in a position to judge how firmly you can trust their estimates. In any event, it starts the project off on the right foot, with you taking the initiative.

3   *What checkpoints are built in to the schedule?*

There should be planned intervals when your department can review the work done to date, request any changes necessary, authorize more work, or even abandon the project, if necessary. The major checkpoints should be after the feasibility study; after detailed systems specifications are completed but *before programming begins*; and when systems testing is finished. Programming is the single most expensive phase of the project; you must satisfy yourself that the system as planned will do what you want it to do before programming starts. Don't let them dazzle you with jargon, either; insist on explanations you can understand.

Beware if the schedule says: 'Friday, finish feasibility study. Monday, get user authorization and begin next phase.' They are giving you no time at all to study the report or ask for changes; an attempt is being made to bamboozle you into giving approval without understanding what is happening.

4   Where are the plans for converting the files?

Especially important if all your files are on paper now, and have to be converted to computer media like tapes and disks. It is a very lengthy and expensive process. For many systems, the file conversion should start well ahead of the planned date for starting the new system. But you need those records to keep the company going on a day-to-day basis; are they planning to move them out of your department for several weeks to do the conversion? Watch out. Who will be checking the new computer files to be sure they're right? There are, no doubt, some errors in the figures now; more will be introduced in keypunching; they have to be found and corrected. It's a long, tedious job. Will it be your responsibility? If so, where will you get the time and the people to do it? Did they think of this when they worked out how much the system was going to cost?

5   What are the plans for training you and your staff?

If you've never had a computer system before, this is particularly important. Everybody will need one or two days on a course on general computer concepts. Then you will need to know all about the day-to-day running of the system. Who fills in the new forms and how? What will the new reports look like and how do you read them? Who corrects errors and how? And if there is a high turnover of staff or if casual labor is used, what about training new people as they come in? Formal sessions should be set up to teach these things, and manuals written for reference. If you don't understand how to run your own system properly the whole project is a waste of time, theirs and yours.

6 *What are the plans for evaluating the system after it's working?*

The only way to be sure the system is working properly is to do a formal evaluation at regular intervals. This should be done by the systems people, and should cover your satisfaction and any changes you would like; the technical efficiency, ie how economical the system is to operate; and a comparison between what it is actually doing and what was proposed in the original feasibility report. (See Chapter 16 for more details.)

7 *Are standards in daily use?*

Methods standards and performance standards. You've got to have the first before you can have the second. Methods standards lay down methods of working for each phase of developing a computer system. For example, for the feasibility study, they should specify the scope of the study, what constitutes the analyst's terms of reference, what should be included in the final report, how the report is turned over to the user management for study, and so on. Performance standards specify the acceptable time and cost for each type of work; for example, how long it should take the average programmer to code and test so many instructions.

Standards are like sex; they're what people in the computer business talk about a lot, but never actually have time for. Everybody's in favor of standards, as long as they don't actually have to use them. *Good* standards make the job easier by setting out the common working procedures for the whole department. It would be a great waste of time if the project team had to spend days discussing the contents of a report; the standards manual can be consulted easily and answer all questions of that sort.

Standards should be flexible, too. One of the most important sections of the manual is the one that describes how to recommend changes. The environment and requirements of the group evolve over a period of time, and the standards have to be changed to keep up. If there is no easy way for the staff to recommend changes, the standards will get out-of-date and no one will use them. There should be a standards manual on every desk in the department, and every one should be well-thumbed; if not, something is wrong with the standards and with department management.

If you *do* get hold of the company's data-processing standards, turn immediately to the sections which describe the reports which you will get during the project. These go by various names: user request (which you should do anyway), feasibility study, systems proposal, systems specifications. If the standards are any good, you'll find each of the reports described—who prepares them, when they are prepared, when you get them, and what they contain. Ask if users were consulted when the standards were written. See if you agree with the contents. Does the report give you all the information you want in a form you can understand?

If they aren't right for you and your project, discuss them with the data processing manager or the project leader before the project goes too far. It's not fair on them if you complain when it's too late. Point out why you want the additional information or the different format.

The next half dozen questions relate to the general management of the computer department. Use them to keep people on their toes, or when you get a funny feeling on the back of your head that all is not well. They may prevent some disasters.

8 *How does his project control system work?*

If he says 'Project what?', his ability as a manager may be in doubt. Basically, project control is a special set of standards—methods standards—for planning a new project and then keeping it on schedule. The details will vary from one company to another, but it should include standard procedures for estimating the length of time a project will require, drawing up and documenting the schedule, progress reports, and progress meetings.

9 What is the formal training plan for data processing staff?

The most likely answer is that there isn't any. Some data-processing departments have absolutely nothing in their budgets for training; others do it on a catch-as-catch-can basis. Formal training is essential. First, it is necessary to give the technicians an understanding of business and business problems—*your* problems —as was mentioned above. The purpose of the computer is to help solve those problems, and the data processing people should have the business background to understand them. A second reason is the fast-changing technology of the computer business. New concepts, new techniques, new equipment are being developed all the time. If you are to get the best possible service from data processing, the computer people have to keep up to date with the latest developments. And finally, if the manager is a promoted technician, he should regularly attend formal courses on management in order to improve his ability.

It is difficult to give rules for how much training is required, because circumstances vary so much. But as a general guide, a new systems analyst, whether he be a promoted programmer or a transfer from another department, should have at least three weeks of formal training in his first year as an analyst. The courses can be given by an outside company or organization, or by the department itself. Thereafter, he should spend at least one week a year at a 'state-of-the-art' seminar, lectures, or special techniques courses. The training should be planned to fit in with his work schedule, and supplemented with on-the-job-training.

You may hear the complaint that training is pointless because people leave so soon. It is ironical that, during the business recession of 1970–1, the first item cut in many computer budgets was training, at a time when the job market was drastically tightening up and for the first time the department had a chance of keeping staff and getting a return on the investment. The most likely reason for a computer person to change his job is to gain new experience—a formal training program helps to *reduce* turnover.

10 *Who is the security officer?*

Not the man who carries the payroll. There should be an individual, inside or outside the data-processing department, with special responsibility for computer security. In a small company he might be a systems analyst who spends only part of his time on this, or the internal auditor. His job includes checking each new system to be sure it has good controls; setting procedures for making copies of important files; teaching staff to challenge strangers they see wandering around; testing the fire alarms and fire extinguishers; and so on.

If the manager tells you there isn't any security officer, start worrying. And insist that a review be done to determine the security needs of the installation. (See Chapter 19 for a more detailed discussion of this problem.)

11 *Where are back-up files kept?*

Copies of key files should be held in a remote location, on the theory that it is very unlikely that two separate disasters will destroy both sets at once. Fire, flood, explosion, riot, hurricane, or earthquake may be unlikely, but every company has insurance on its computer just in case. You can't insure data easily; if the worst happens, the company may go out of business if it doesn't have copies of important files. Fifty per cent of all companies that lose their accounts in a fire and don't have copies go into bankruptcy.

Further questions to ask: Are copies of transactions kept too? What about security at the storage location—could the files be stolen? Are they kept in a fire-proof safe? Are there environmental controls, regulated temperature, and humidity as in the home computer room? Have the files ever been retrieved in an emergency practice run?

12 *What percentage of computer time is spent on re-runs, and who pays for it?*

If the computer manager doesn't know and can't find out, the department really is in trouble. Efficient running of the computer itself is all-important. A 're-run' happens when something goes wrong with a production run and it has to be done over again. This can happen because the operator made a mistake—for example, by putting up the wrong file; because there was a bug in the program or in the software; because the input was wrong or not all there and nobody spotted it in time; or because something goes physically wrong with some piece of the equipment. Most of these can be prevented, but unless the manager knows how often they are happening and how much it is costing he can't improve things.

13 *Is the console log reviewed every day? Is it really?*

The console log is the continuous roll of paper in the typewriter of the computer. All work being done is automatically logged on the typewriter. It will show, for example, if the same job was run twice (re-runs), how long each job took, and how long the computer just sat there waiting for someone to tell it what to do next. The computer operators should keep a separate, hand-written log, where they add their own comments about why a re-run was necessary, etc. The two should be compared every day, and any discrepancies checked out. Every minute of computer time, from when it was turned on in the morning to when it's turned off at night (if it ever is) must be accounted for. Computers are too expensive to fool around with.

One objective of this is to see how efficiently the machine is being used, and to see if improvements can be made, as was shown in Embarrassing Question number 6. Another reason is to keep the computer operators honest. Oh, you trust them? You trust the company accountant too, but you have auditors who satisfy themselves that the books balance. One company which trusted its operators found, after several years, that the boys on the night shift always left the computer on and idling when they went home at night. The day shift covered for them. The two groups split the overtime pay the night shift got for all the 'extra time' they put in. In another company, the computer operators were *selling* time on the machine to their friends and pocketing the money. Management never knew. In both cases, a simple check of the console log against the work that was supposed to have been done would have prevented the frauds.

Don't be afraid of making yourself unpopular with these questions. The long-term results can only be better computer systems, which is to everyone's benefit.

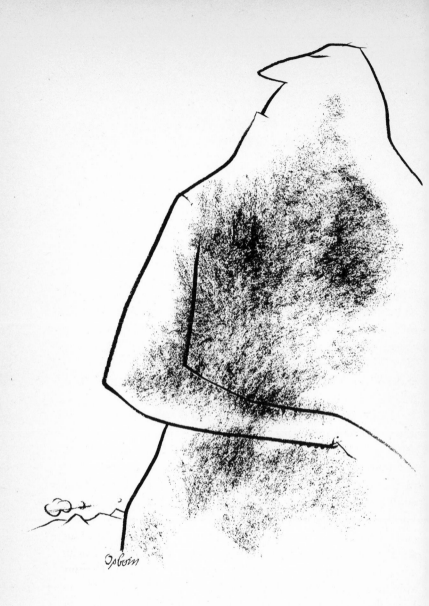

24

The View from the Top

This chapter takes the view of the management at the top of the company. Imagine you're the guy at the top ultimately responsible for corporate objectives, policy, and strategy. (Or maybe you already are.) To support you, you have your senior managers. The company has a policy for production, marketing, personnel, and so on. You hope it will also have a policy for computer usage.

The general policy in some companies is expressed in a single edict: '*We will use a computer*'. This can have a number of effects, some good and some bad. In one company, for example, this policy was taken to absurd lengths; no money could be spent on methods or procedures unless they were computer-based. One engineer wanted a new desk calculator, value $250. No joy. He then requested an all-singing, all-dancing computer terminal, cost $6,000, which was supplied with no hesitation at all. Under such a policy, there may be resentment of or reaction against computers. Certainly, a uniform policy is necessary. Computer systems can cut across departmental or divisional lines, and it is here that co-ordination and top management policy becomes important. Centralization of data can imply a deeper centralization of other functions.

Any company using computers must have some sort of long

term plan, supported at the highest level. Some companies have developed a detailed plan for five years ahead based on a complete review of business and information needs. (Such a survey in a big company can take three years or more with a result that the plan is out of date before the ink is dry.) The plan should be a framework which can be used for setting priorities and assessing individual projects (user requests) initiated by lower management.

Evaluation of projects against the plan and a watching brief on progress is sometimes the role of a Computer Steering Committee. This is composed of the appropriate senior and line managers, and, of course, data processing management.

The chairman of the Steering Committee, when it comes to policy, must be the top man. There is the danger that if the data processing manager or management services manager is too low down in the organization (say, two levels or more below the financial director), some of the senior management will be spending too much time in project details. The data processing manager should have authority equal to that of computer user management in the organizational hierarchy.

One aspect of computing which requires a senior management decision is who pays for computer development and operational work. This can be a major bone of contention between users and data processing. There are as many policies and methods for charging computing work as there are large computer users. Some companies don't charge development work or computer time back to users, all expenditure being a general company overhead. Others charge only for computer operation.

Charging users for all computer work imposes a discipline on selecting applications, and on the way in which the development is carried out. One large company with decentralized operating divisions and centralized computing facilities tried different policies and methods. It provides a useful case study.

1. Objective: Get users to use the computer. Each of the divisions was charged equally with recovering the entire data processing budget. Because they were paying for the computer

work, they might as well get something for it. Howls of mutiny came from the divisions. The plan was abandoned.

2.   Objective: Get people to use the computer, but in a disciplined manner. Each division was charged for development and running costs of work done. The total operations budget was divided by available machine hours to get the rate. This was then charged out according to hours used. (What happens to unallocated hours? Does the cost come down as more work goes on the machine?) The charge was deducted from each division's profits. Result: The most prosperous divisions used the computer. Those that were struggling with a poor cash position, had most need of the computer but couldn't afford it. The company is still limping along with this policy. Better guidance from top management is needed.

Decisions on charging for computer work must be made at the highest level. Using charging as a stick to force people to use the computer doesn't work, but care must be taken that the method is equitable and agreeable to all.

You can assess your firm's computing efforts by answering the following questions:

— Are you satisfied that your company is getting a good return on the money invested in computer projects?
— Are there good relations between data processing and users?
— Do *you* benefit from the computing facilities?
— Accepting that data processing may have to be an internal monopoly, how does the department measure itself?
— Are your data processing people in touch with commercial reality?

If you have doubts about computing in your company, remember the First Law: Computerization is doomed if it is to be used by bad management. It's useless to spend money on sophisticated management reports if management isn't capable of using them.

Glossary

Access time. The time that elapses between giving an instruction to access a storage location and the moment when the transfer of data to or from that area begins.

Address. The reference number which uniquely identifies an area of computer storage.

ALGOL. A high-level programming language designed for scientific/technical use. Derived from ALGOrithmic Language.

Algorithm. A sequence of statements defining a computational procedure.

Analog computer. A computer which stores and processes numeric quantities which are represented by physical quantities (such as voltage, resistance etc).

Assembler. A computer program which operates on a source program (qv) written in an assembly language (qv).

Assembly language. A symbolic language used by programmers which is then converted (by an assembler (qv) program) to machine-code that the computer can store and execute.

BASIC. A high level programming language, principally for mathematical calculations. Derived from *B*eginners *A*ll-purpose *S*ymbolic *I*nstruction *C*ode.

Batch. An accumulation of data to be processed; for example, all the time-cards for a department may represent a batch of input.

Batch-processing. A system in which data is accumulated to form a batch, the batches being processed at regular intervals. For example, all orders are accumulated during the day, everyday, and processed in the evening. Contrast with real-time processing.

Binary. A number system which is based on counting in twos; forms the basis for holding data in a modern digital computer. Numbers are held as a pattern of os and 1s. A o is normally represented by physical conditions such as 'no pulse', 'no-magnetism' etc, a 1 being represented by 'pulse', 'magnetized'.

Bit. A contraction of *BI*nary digi*T*; a single value of 'o' or '1' in a binary (qv) number.

Block. 1. A unit of information of convenient size for processing. 2. The area of storage in which a block of information is recorded.

Branch, conditional. Also known as a conditional jump. A computer instruction which can be used to vary the sequence in which program instructions are obeyed by the computer. A branch instruction tests a condition within the computer (such as: are two values equal?) and based on the result (yes or no) the machine will execute one of two sequences of program instructions. See also control, transfer of.

Branch, unconditional. Also known as an unconditional jump. A computer instruction which causes the sequence in which the instructions are obeyed to be automatically changed. See also control, transfer of.

Buffer. A temporary storage area which is used to equalize or balance the different operating speeds. For example, a buffer can be used between a slow input device, such as a typewriter, and the main computer (central processor) which operates at very high speed. The input device would be said to be 'buffered'.

Bug. An error—in program, data, or system. Hence debugging—removing errors.

Byte. A unit of computer storage consisting of eight bits (qv).

Card punch. 1. A device which accepts information from the computer's memory (qv) (internal storage) and punches it into cards. 2. A keyboard device by which an operator can punch cards, also known as a key punch.

Card reader. A device which reads information punched into cards. The information read is transfered into the computer's memory (qv) (internal storage).

Central processor unit (CPU). The main part of the computer consisting of the memory (qv) (internal storage, control unit, arithmetic unit and operating console). Peripherals (qv) are linked to the CPU. Also known as 'the main frame'.

Character. One of the set of symbols that can be used by a particular data processing system, such as the numbers 0 to 9, the letters A to Z and additional symbols $(+-''/\$)$, etc.

Check digit. A method of ensuring that certain data items entering the computer system are valid. A special character—the check digit—is generated for a data value and appended to it. The computer checks that the combination of data value and check digit is valid.

COBOL. A high level programming language, based on English-type statements, for general commercial use. Derived from COmmon Business Oriented Language.

Compiler. A special processor program which operates on a source program, written by the programmer to turn it into a machine-code (object) program which can be executed by the computer.

Console. The main control unit used by the (human) computer operators. In old machines, a switch panel; in current machines, a typewriter. The console typewriter enables operator to communicate with computer and vice versa, by means of simple messages.

Control total. A method for checking that a batch of data is complete, or a computer file has been processed satisfactorily. Example: User counts number of documents in a batch; documents again counted as they are received for processing, number of punch cards produced are counted, number of cards read by the computer are counted. Checks of these total counts are made at each stage to ensure that the volumes of data balance.

Control, transfer of. Computer instructions, forming a program, are normally obeyed in the sequence in which they are stored. Special instructions, called branch instructions (conditional and unconditional) (qv) enable the sequence in which instructions are obeyed to be varied.

Core. A term, becoming obsolete, for the internal storage in the central processor unit (qv). (Derived from a form of storage which consisted of a large number of magnetizable rings called cores.)

Decision table. A tabular method for recording conditional procedures of the format 'if . . . then . . .'

Diagnostics. Commonly, a listing of program errors which is produced by a compiler (qv) or assembler (qv).

Digital computer. A computer which handles data in numeric form. Information is held in binary (qv) form, with electronic switches recording os and 1s. Contrast with analog computer (qv).

Direct access. A store, usually a magnetic disk or drum, which is divided into a number of addressable areas. Data can be put on the device or read from the device by quoting the appropriate address (qv). This means that data can be stored or retrieved without serial searching.

Edit. To check the correctness of data, and to change as necessary the form of data, adding or deleting certain characters. For example, part of program can edit data for printing, adding special symbols (such as $.), spacing, deleting nonsignificant zeros, etc.

Encode. 1. Generally, any process in which data in one form is recoded to a different form. 2. Specifically, to transcribe data from documents to magnetic tape using an operator-controlled keyboard device.

Exchangeable disk. The most popular form of direct access (qv) device. The basic recording media is a stack of disks forming a portable disk pack which the operator can load or unload on the disk drive (reading/writing unit) as required. Example: a disk pack might consist of eleven disks, 14 inches in diameter, mounted on a central spindle. The pack would weigh about 10 lbs and hold some 29 million characters of data.

Executive. Synonym for operating systems (qv).

Field. A portion of a peripheral (qv) storage media, or internal storage, or a document used to hold one item of data.

File. An organized collection of information, e.g. a series of records (qv) stored in key (qv) number sequence.

Fixed disk. A direct access storage device, consisting of one or more large disks permanently fixed in a disk drive unit. Example: One unit has four disks, $26\frac{1}{2}$ inches in diameter, which can hold 10 million characters of data; average access time (qv) is 20 milliseconds.

Flag. A symbol used to mark a record for special attention. Example: on a listing (qv) of a program, all statements which contain errors may be flagged for the attention of the programmer.

Flowchart. A diagrammatic representation of a procedure or program which shows its conditional logic. For example, a flowchart of a program will show unconditional branches by means of diamonds and actions by means of rectangles.

FORTRAN. A high level language used for scientific or technical programs. Derived from *FOR*mula *TRAN*slation.

Hardware. Physical units of equipment.

Hexadecimal. A number system which is based on counting in sixteens. Used in many third-generation computers. Digits greater than '9' are represented by letters of the alphabet.

Housekeeping. The general organizational activities necessary to maintain control of a process.

Indexed sequential. A means of organizing data on a direct access (qv) device (in key [qv] sequence). A directory or index is created to show where the data records are stored. Any desired data record can thus be retrieved from the device by consulting the index(es).

Instruction. A group of characters (or bits) that defines an operation to be performed by the computer.

Jump. Synonym for branch (qv).

Justify. To align the characters in a field. For example, to left justify, the first character (e.g. the most significant digit) appears in the leftmost character position in a field. To right justify, the last character (e.g. the least significant digit) is written in the last or rightmost character position in the field.

K. A thousand, or approximately a thousand. For example, a computer man could say his machine is '32K'. This means the memory (qv) can hold a maximum of 32,000 units of storage (e.g. characters, bytes or words).

Key. A field (qv) which contains a code that uniquely identifies a record. For example, in a personnel file, with one record for each employee, each record will be identified by a unique code: the employee number.

Label. 1. A legible note attached to an exchangeable disk (qv) pack or magnetic tape reel to enable the operator to identify it. 2. One or two blocks (qv) recorded on a peripheral storage medium (disk or tape) which enables the program to identify it. 3. A field (qv) in a source program (qv) which enables the programmer to refer to a statement (e.g. for a branch [qv]).

Line printer. An output peripheral (qv) device which prints data one line at a time.

Listing. Generally, any report produced on a line printer which is not printed on special pre-printed paper. For example, a source listing is a print-out of the source program (qv) processed by the compiler (qv); an error listing is a report showing all input data found to be invalid by the processing program.

Loop. A series of computer instructions arranged in such a manner that the machine repeats a series of operations automatically until a terminal condition is reached.

Magnetic disk. A peripheral (qv) storage device in which data is recorded on magnetizable disk surfaces. See exchangeable disk, fixed disk and direct access.

Magnetic drum. A peripheral storage device consisting of cylinder with a magnetizable surface on which data is recorded; this is a direct access (qv) device.

Magnetic tape. A plastic-based tape, coated with a magnetizable substance, on which data can be recorded and retrieved by a peripheral (qv) unit called magnetic tape drive. The tapes are loaded on and unloaded from the drive as required.

Memory. The internal storage in the central processor unit (qv) of the computer.

MICR. *M*agnetic *I*nk *C*haracter *R*ecognition. Characters printed in a special type-face using ink containing magnetizable particles. Can be read by both machines and people. Commonly used on bank checks.

Microsecond. One one-millionth part of a second (10^{-6} second) abbreviated μs, or microsec.

Millisecond. One one-thousanth part of a second (10^{-3} second), abbreviated ms, or millisec.

Module. Specifically, one logical part of a program. A major program may be broken down into a number of logically self-contained modules. These modules may be written (and tested) separately, possibly by a number of programmers (one module per programmer). The modules can then be put together to form the complete program. This is called modular programming.

Multiprocessing. The technique whereby two or more programs operate in the computer at the same time, each with its own place in memory, but each having its own CPU. Cf Multiprogramming (qv).

Multiprogramming. The technique of operating two or more programs in a computer at the same time. Each program is alloted its own place in memory and its own peripherals (qv), but all share the CPU. Made economical by the fact that peripherals are slower than the CPU, so most programs spend most of their time waiting for input or output to finish. While one program is waiting, another can use the CPU.

Nanosecond. One-thousandth-millionth part of a second (10^{-9} second), abbreviated as ns, or nanosec.

Object program. The machine-code program which can be executed by the computer produced from the automatic translation of a source program (qv).

OCR. Optical *C*haracter *R*ecognition. Characters printed in a special type style which can be read by both machines and people.

Off-line. A process not carried out by the computer or a device not directly linked to the central processor unit (qv) or its peripherals (qv).

On-line. Any process carried out by the computer or a unit linked to or under the control of any part of the computer. The opposite of off-line.

Operating system. A master control program which performs many housekeeping operations. It is available to the computer at all times either being held in memory (qv) or on a peripheral (qv) storage device.

Packing density. The amount of information which can be recorded in a given space. For example the packing density of a magnetic disk or tape is usually given in bpi—bits (qv) per inch.

Paper tape. A basic input medium. It consists of a continuous strip of paper in which information is recorded in the form of coded holes. Example: 8-track paper tape is 1″ wide and a character is recorded by punching a code of up to eight holes across the width of tape. Could be prepared by a typewriter keyboard device, or as a by-product to some other activity (such as a cash register) or by a special peripheral punching device attached to the central processor unit (qv).

Parameter. A variable value, which is given to a program before it is run.

Peripheral. A device which is connected to the central processor unit (qv):
— input device enables data to be input to the CPU
— output device enables data to be output from the CPU

— file storage device enables mass data to be stored; data is put on the device from the CPU and retrieved into the CPU.

PL/1. *P*rogramming *L*anguage One. A high-level programming language developed by IBM.

Program. 1. (noun) The complete series of instructions for a job to be performed on the computer. Once the program is loaded and started the computer will automatically obey the instructions. 2. (verb) To devise the set of instructions of a program.

Programming language. A symbolic language in which a programmer codes a program. The programmer prepares a source program (qv) using the programming language and this is then converted to the machine-code object program (qv) by means of a special processing program (a compiler [qv] or assembler [qv]). A high-level programming language is one which is biased towards the human programmer. An assembly language (qv) is a lower-level language being a compromise between the way the computer holds an instruction and ease of use by the programmer.

Punched card. A basic input medium: a card of high quality material in which data is recorded by punching coded-hole patterns. Example: standard card measures approximately $7\frac{3}{8}''$ x $3\frac{1}{4}''$ x .007″ and consists of eighty vertical columns each column holding one character of information. Prepared by a card punch (qv); information is input to the central processor unit (qv) by means of a card reader (qv).

Read. To get information from any input or file storage media. For example, reading punched cards by detecting the pattern of holes, or reading a magnetic tape by sensing the patterns of magnetism.

Record. A group or block of related data treated as a record. See file (qv) and key (qv).

Real time. The processing of data for immediate use in controlling the activities at the data source. (Contrast with batch-processing [qv].) Most often quoted example is airline seat reservations: a customer booking enquiry is entered into the computer to see if space is available. If a seat is booked, the file of available seats is updated immediately, thus giving an up-to-date record of seats reserved and seats available.

Routine. Sometimes used as a synonym for program. Can be used to mean any part of a program that deals with the particular aspects of the overall procedure. See also sub-routine.

Run. The performance of a complete computer program through to its end condition.

Sequential processing. Reading, and/or writing (qv), records of a file, one by one, in ascending key (qv) sequence.

Serial processing. Reading, and/or writing (qv), records of file, one by one, in the physical sequence in which they are stored.

Software. 1. Any program. 2. A program or group of programs which is supplied, pre-written, and pre-tested, by a contractor.

Sort. 1. (verb) To arrange records according to a logical system. Nowadays, most sorting is done on the computer using magnetic disks, drums, or tapes. 2. (noun) A utility (qv) program which sorts records held on disk or tape.

Source program. The program prepared by the programmer using a special, symbolic programming language. It is converted to the machine-code object program (qv) by a special processing program, a compiler (qv) or assembler (qv).

Sub-routine. A self-contained unit of program coding which performs one complete task. Many sub-routines are supplied, pre-written, and tested by an outside agency, and can be slotted into a program as required.

Terminal. A peripheral (qv) on-line to the computer, but remote from it; in the next room, another city, or another country. Usually for input or output from or for a human being (rather than another computer) but can be for input or output of punched cards, magnetic tape etc.

Third generation. The current generation of computers, built after 1964, characterized by solid-state circuitry and complicated software to perform many functions. Cf: Second generation: computers of the era 1957–64, characterized by transistors and core (qv) memories, many still in operation. First generation: pre-1957 computers, characterized by mercury delay lines and vacuum tubes. Now museum pieces.

Track. A path along which data is recorded on a continuous or rotational medium, such as paper tape, magnetic tape, a magnetic disk or drum.

Utility. A program used for repetitive data-handling procedures, such as sorting, transcribing data from one peripheral medium to another. (Usually pre-written and tested software (qv).)

Update. To revise a master file in respect of current information or transactions.

Validation. The examination of data (possibly by computer program) for correctness against certain criteria, such as format (patterns of numbers, spaces, and letters) ranges (upper and lower value limits), check digits (qv), equivalent entries on a master file. Also known as a data vet.

*VDU. V*isual *D*isplay *U*nit. An output (or input/output) peripheral device on which data is displayed on some type of screen.

Virtual storage. An old concept recently made commercially feasible, whereby large quantities of data (up to 100s of millions of characters) are held on mass storage devices (disks) and made available to the CPU as if held in memory. The computer 'doesn't know' whether the data comes from its own memory or a peripheral (qv).

Word. A basic unit of storage in a computer, consisting of a number of bits. The word length (number of bits [qv] per word) may be fixed or variable depending on the type. of computer.

Write. To record information on a peripheral medium, e.g. to record data onto a magnetic disk or tape.

Epilogue

From all the systems we've seen—the successes and the failures—and all the users and computer technicians we've dealt with, we have tried to reduce all the do's and don'ts to ten golden rules. If you follow these rules, we can't guarantee that your computer system will be successful, but we are certain that it won't be an abject failure.

1   Define the aims of the system

Set down in black and white what you want the new system to achieve. The best system objectives are those against which the implemented system can subsequently be judged by asking the question: 'have we succeeded?'

2   Don't be too optimistic

A computer technician will double the benefits and halve the costs to justify a system. It is more realistic to halve the benefits and double the costs.

3   Analyze, don't just synthesize

Avoid the temptation of designing or approving a system which is technically elegant—and then inventing the problems that the system could solve. Identify the aims of the system, identify the problem areas—and then solve the problems.

4   Use the so what? test

When a new management report is proposed or claims are made for the information reporting aspects of the computer system, apply the *so what?* test. 'This new system will give a breakdown of all sales made, by area, within twenty-four hours'—reaction: 'SO WHAT?' 'This costing report will show the distribution of labor costs, by department, for every dollar earnt in revenue'—'SO WHAT?' This is the acid test; it will help refine your reporting requirements and pinpoint useless reports before money is wasted on producing them.

5   Look at the system in the context of the business as a whole

Be certain in your own mind what the system *won't* do. There are many external factors which won't be specifically reported from the computer system; the state of the market, the percentage of the market that your company has, the form of the competition, the changes in the economic climate that affects your products, and so on. No computer can make all the right decisions at the right time. It is a tool to help you—not an end in its own right. Also, remember the Bob Smiths of business.

6   Use the what if . . .? test

When looking at the design of a proposed system, identify the weakest points and most important assumptions. Then ask *what if . . .?* to test whether the system is realistic and flexible. 'Stock requisitions will be received by 16.00 hours and processed by the computer after they have been punched'—reaction: 'what if they are delayed beyond 16.00, what if there are errors, what if the computer isn't available' etc.

7   *Remember the '80/20' rule in computer systems*

This is a good general rule which applies in many areas of developing a computer system. To forget or ignore it may mean that you spend a lot of money for only a little return. For example, 80 per cent of the system development and operating costs go into only 20 per cent of the data—the errors and exceptions; 80 per cent of the benefits of the system can come from 20 per cent of the processing. In many stock control systems employing sophisticated statistical techniques, the majority of the benefits come from just looking at the range of stock movement on every product every day; the statistical processing may give only small, marginal benefits.

8.   *The success of the system will be limited—or helped—by the quality of the management*

No amount of computerization will really help a company which has basically poor management: management to whom planning is an anethema, which refuses even to specify objectives, or which has let bad industrial relations develop, and so on. Never attempt to use the computer as an excuse to implement management or organizational changes, hoping that the new ideas will solve or cover up problems which are endemic in the company.

9   *Plan*

Look ahead to the work that has to be done in developing the system, and the changes which are likely to arise in the future. Planning is especially important in implementing the new system: don't imagine that the work is over when you approve the design. Try to determine what is likely to change in your environment after the system goes in: a system designed for today could collapse tomorrow.

10 *Don't opt out*

Sure, computers are technical, you've got your job to do, some computer people like to get on with the job without your 'interference'.

Remember that your computer people may not be in touch with business reality and they must capitalize on your experience. You will have to live with the system, possibly for years. Ensure that checkpoints are incorporated into the development schedule so that you can review the work before too much money is spent.